WOMEN
in
TRANSITION

NAVIGATING THE LEGAL AND FINANCIAL

CHALLENGES IN YOUR LIFE

PEGGY R. HOYT, J.D., M.B.A.

AND CANDACE M. POLLOCK, J.D.

WOMEN IN TRANSITION

NAVIGATING THE LEGAL AND FINANCIAL CHALLENGES IN YOUR LIFE

ISBN 0-9719177-5-2

Copyright © 2006 by Peggy R. Hoyt and Candace M. Pollock

Published by Legacy Planning Partners, LLC
254 Plaza Drive
Oviedo, Florida 32765
Phone (407) 977-8080
Facsimile (407) 977-8078
www.BeAnAuthor.com

Printed in the United States of America.

DEDICATION

*Our society still embraces the "happily ever after" dream—
not just for women, but for everyone: We meet soul mates, have
important, rewarding careers, loving children and fulfilling activities.
Unfortunately, real life can throw us a curve ball and
everything we worked hard for can be in jeopardy or just
different than we anticipated.*

*This book is dedicated to women who have faced life's
curve balls and have had the agility and fortitude to undergo the
metamorphosis from the life of a caterpillar to that of a butterfly.*

For more information or to order a copy of this book,
visit www.WomenInTransitionToday.com
or call 407.977.8080 or 216.861.6160

The publishing of this book should not be construed as legal, accounting or other professional advice. If legal advice or other professional services are needed or required, please seek the services of a licensed, competent professional.

The hiring of a lawyer is an important decision that should not be based solely upon advertisements. Before you decide, ask us to send you free written information about our qualifications and experience.

Book Design by Julie Hoyt Dorman
www.dormangraphics.com

TABLE of CONTENTS

fOREWARD

Women in Transition is written for every woman as she moves from one phase of life to another ~ living with parents, on her own, living in a committed relationship (marriage or otherwise), experiencing widowhood or divorce, followed by relationships thereafter or on her own again. Each transition presents potential areas of vulnerability with personal, legal and financial lessons, opportunities and challenges. Women take the experience (lessons they learn or fail to learn) and resources (personal, financial and legal) at each phase as the foundation for the next phase. This foundation is either shaky or solid and contributes to or undermines her success, security, and independence thereafter.

This book is intended to give women a roadmap to legal and financial protections, security, and opportunities they can create for themselves as they transition from one life phase to another—whether the transition is by choice or fate. It provides a "how to" process about how a woman can protect herself. Failure to do so can make or break her future security.

We encourage you to share your thoughts, concerns, insights and suggestions by visiting *www.WomenInTransitionToday.com.*

chapter one

Women in Transition

Women are at their most vulnerable and are most likely to lose opportunities when they fail to create and update legal and financial strategies—when they transition from one phase of life to another. Life is full of numerous cruel realities for women whether they realize it or not. Some of these cruel facts are obvious. Others are more subtle, so they do not seem to apply or do not catch a woman's attention and she is complacent about taking steps to overcome the threats to her security. Statistics show, for instance, that women are:

- More likely to earn less than men in the same industries;
- More likely to postpone home ownership until they are in a committed relationship (marriage or otherwise) although the percentage of single women home owners has increased 3% from 1997 to 2003 according to the National Association of Realtors;
- Postponing marriage until their thirties or forties;
- More likely than men to postpone or interrupt their careers in order to raise a family;
- More likely to experience compromises in their earning capacity and career advancement when opting for flexible work schedules while raising their family;
- More likely than men to file for bankruptcy following divorce or upon the death of a spouse, even if they are career women;
- Enjoying longer life spans than males, bringing women to an average lifespan of 82.6 yrs; (2005 Credit Suisse Longevity Index by Credit Suisse First Boston LLC);
- More likely to die single according to the Women's Institute for a Secure Retirement;
- More likely (90% per The Department of Labor) to be solely responsible for their financial well-being at some point in their lives;

- More likely to place their financial needs and independence behind the needs of their family; and
- Less likely to have sufficient retirement funds in place to adequately support themselves over their lifetimes.

A study by the Center For Human Resource Research at Ohio State University published in the Journal of Sociology in 2006 on the connection between marital status and net worth revealed some statistics that are important for women facing divorce or widowhood:

- Married individuals build greater net worth and do so faster than single or divorced individuals (annual growth of net worth for married individuals was 16% versus 8% and 14%, respectively, for single or divorced individuals);
- Married individuals have a 93% higher net worth than single or divorced individuals;
- Divorced individuals lose approximately 75% of their net worth even when the property settlement divides assets equally;
- Overall, men have greater financial security than women.

What do these statistics mean for women? ***Women need to do more with less over a longer period of time and they need to plan for the likelihood of flying solo, by choice or fate, just in case.*** As a result of bias, socialization, lack of experience or a number of other factors, as a group, women have more impediments to achieving and maintaining financial security than men. They can wait and hope that they are in the statistical minority and they can only deal with things if and when a crisis occurs. Or, they can methodically invest in their financial-legal literacy, acquiring knowledge and skills that will give them confidence and independence and place them in the best possible position should they fall into the statistical majority.

These statements do not mean that larger groups of women are not financially successful and sophisticated. It merely means that women, as a *statistical* group, are more vulnerable than men and need to calculate the impact that longer life spans, lower pay scales and other factors have on their security and confidence. They need to take extra steps to ensure that at least the core protections are in place so they, and the people and things they cherish, are less vulnerable to financial, legal and other challenges they might face.

Unfortunately, most media directed at women tends to give more advice and attention to helping women update their wardrobes or home décor than to educating them about legal and financial protections—especially as they move from one life phase to another. Even magazines catering to young career women don't normally carry substantive articles about the importance of healthcare proxies or the legal implications of different forms of asset ownership.

Financial brokerage firms provide legal-financial information to their customers but many women don't routinely deal with such firms and, therefore, are not regular recipients of this information. Some women might participate in a 401(k) program at work, but many traditionally "female" occupations have limited opportunities in this regard. Nonetheless, many women choose financial vehicles on the more conservative end of the financial spectrum with corresponding conservative returns. They might not venture into financial vehicles with which they are not familiar even though these investment choices can be relatively safe and produce a greater overall return over time.

Occasional news headlines such as those associated with the Terry Schiavo matter regarding end of life decision making will motivate some people to take action regarding estate planning but not necessarily in a holistic way. There are few on-going mechanisms in place to expose young women, single women, married women, divorced women and widowed women– in a nutshell—all women, to the information they need to remain financially and legally viable and safe.

Women who don't have easy access to financial-legal input must initiate and sustain the learning process on their own to collect the information they need. This is not likely to happen in our fast-paced and demanding lives—especially if life involves responsibility for children, aging parents, work, home-keeping and maintaining a committed relationship—all on top of community or other activities. Who has time left to spend on financial and legal education?!

Plus, there is just no easy way to get a good, impartial overview of the information everyone should have for baseline protections. The good news is there is a lot of information available via the Internet and other sources. The bad news is there is a lot of information available and it is not always easy to sift out the good information from the bad, and the disguised sales pitch. Consequently, women, like most people, often deal with what life throws at them without a sense that they can direct some of their own destiny. This can contribute to an ambient anxiety that keeps women from taking action. This leads to what Liz Perle, author of *Money: A Memoir*, quantifies as "anxiety plus insecurity equals avoidance." Many people, not just women, play ostrich and avoid taking action to ensure their legal and financial security. Given the above statistics, however, women face much greater risks to their autonomy and viability.

It is easy enough to be somewhat oblivious to the legal or financial underpinnings of daily experience when a woman moves from phase to phase in her life. We all can live somewhat naively about our financial and legal vulnerability unless we experience a mishap that contributes to our experience bank. Many of these mishaps can be relatively benign. Perhaps a woman gets stuck with an expensive apartment lease when a roommate moves out or she gets over-extended on a credit account. She can feel the financial pain, learn some important lessons and move on. How well she learns these valuable life lessons will dictate whether she is likely to repeat this cycle.

However, most women begin to realize over time that she should create some protections in order to weather challenges and take advantage of opportunities in life. This might come about because there is an underlying sense of unease about "what might happen." Or, she might not always understand *how* to take action but understand she needs to do *something* ~ whether she is in a relationship or not. She knows that she is ultimately responsible for her own well-being and safety—financially, legally and otherwise.

Women in Transition explores a woman's life—in all its potential phases—from leaving home, to entering into a committed relationship, to choosing life as a single, to ending up single by fate, to retirement, along with all the possible crises that might evolve at each phase. Each phase presents its own unique opportunities and challenges. Join us on this journey to explore legal and financial strategies to create wealth, protect wealth, attain wealth independence and, ultimately, leave a wealth legacy. We look forward to the experience.�֍

chapter two

The Confidence Continuum ™

The following chapters explain the steps every woman needs to take to secure her autonomy and security—financially and legally. However, it is important to organize this information around a useful framework to aid comprehension about how the important pieces of information and strategies fit together. We call that framework THE CONFIDENCE CONTINUUM™. The Confidence Continuum is a graphical representation of the natural components or stages needed to establish financial and legal safety and confidence. Understanding where a legal or financial decision or opportunity fits into a particular phase of a woman's life should make it easier to understand where and how gaps or conflicts might exist in her legal and financial protections. A woman's confidence, safety and independence will be tied to how well she has coordinated her financial and legal strategies with her phase of life.

THE CONFIDENCE CONTINUUM™

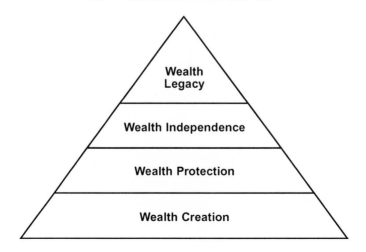

Wealth Creation represents the phase of earning income, managing money, acquiring assets that increase in value over time, and maintaining a manageable level of debt—all of the basic foundation steps most of us take when we begin to make our way in the world. We start with these foundational steps and build upon that base step-by-step. Eventually, we have the core financial pieces in place which we thereafter need to protect.

Wealth Protection represents a phase in which we utilize legal and financial strategies to minimize loss of the assets (wealth) we have accumulated and to maximize the likelihood that those assets will increase in value to continue to meet our goals. Wealth is not just our monetary assets. Wealth also includes the people and things we cherish such as family and pets, and quality-of-life matters such as autonomy and activities. This phase represents the steps and strategies we implement to protect our assets for ourselves and those we love, including times when we cannot communicate our wishes due to disability or death.

Wealth Independence represents the phase where the core financial vehicles have produced sufficient financial heft to offer a woman a measure of financial freedom and independence. For example, in this phase a woman is well insured against financial loss due to natural disaster, business reversal, loss of her spouse or partner from death or divorce or other unexpected catastrophic financial events. She is no longer living pay check to pay check. Her legal and financial planning give her the wherewithal to maintain autonomy under most circumstances.

Wealth Legacy represents the phase where a woman is in a position to create a lasting legacy that leaves not only her valuables, but also her values, for others as well as the causes she supports. Her financial and legal strategies are designed to help her lead by example and contribute to others through her experience and lessons she can share.

A woman can move through The Confidence Continuum depending on effort, sophistication and events in life. In fact, she can be in various stages of evolution at any one time depending on how complex her financial and legal goals and life situation might be. For example, she might have been on her own for a while, have a savings account and has begun to invest in a retirement account but she might have such large debt that she is jeopardizing her financial safety. She would need to create protections to insulate the wealth she has created against her outstanding debt before she can move up along The Confidence Continuum toward greater wealth independence, confidence and competence.

The following chapters will refer to The Confidence Continuum as we talk about a woman's evolution through the most common phases of life. Keep in mind that The Confidence Continuum is not intended as a value judgment about whether a woman needs to accumulate a specified level of wealth. Like beauty, wealth is in the eye of the beholder. The point is that a plan for creating financial and legal security exists whether a woman actively creates her plan or one develops by default. Every woman will decide for herself—and, we hope, with the input of her trusted advisors—what is achievable and consistent with her goals and circumstances. Wealth is merely a means to an end—increasing confidence and security regardless of what life throws at us.

chapter Three

Wealth   Creation

As a young woman approaches the age of 18 and high school graduation, there are a several decisions that she needs to make. Will she go to college or begin a career? Will she have a traditional forty hour workweek type of job, pursue a career in the military or remain at home caring for a family? Will she remain in her parents' home for a while or indefinitely after school, or will she venture out to establish her own home? The answers to these and other life-defining questions will determine the course for her future. There are no right or wrong answers, only the answers that work for her.

It is sometimes hard to fathom that a college education was not always an option for women. It wasn't too long ago that a college education for a woman wasn't assumed the way it is now for a majority of young women graduating from high school. Some families couldn't afford post high school education or justify it for their daughters. Many women, who are now in their fifties, sixties and beyond, were raised at a time when it was assumed that men would get a higher education so they could get a good job and support their families. Women were expected to remain at home to rear children and maintain the home. Those who did work were often expected to quit their jobs when they married or at least while the children were in school. We've come a long way baby, as they say! Today, most colleges boast enrollments in near equal numbers of men to women. Women outnumber men in numerous law, medical and other professional schools.

Historically, some professions have been traditionally female dominated and some were male dominated. Women were expected to become teachers, nurses, or beauticians. Men became doctors, lawyers, construction workers and salespeople. These distinctions don't exist as strongly as before. It is just as common today to see a woman judge as it is a man; a female doctor and a male nurse. Women are present on almost every construction site in America today.

As mentioned in Chapter One, statistics show women still earn only approximately seventy-five cents to a man's dollar in many occupations. Women also still experience the "glass ceiling" when it comes to promotion to the highest level management positions.

A discussion about the reasons or sources of these differences is beyond the scope of this book. But, it is important to understand that some of these factors influence whether and how women will be able to live with confidence and security at any stage in life. Whether a young woman remains in her parents' home or leaves it to be on her own in whatever form requires that she have a number of financial and legal strategies and tools available, not only for survival but to help her thrive. Generally at this stage, young women are just entering the wealth creation phase of The Confidence Continuum.

Establishing a separate financial and Legal identity

The first thing a woman needs to do is establish a financial and legal identity separate from her parents, after reaching the legal age of majority at 18 years. The sooner she does this, the sooner she can truly call herself an "emancipated" adult and begin to reap the benefits of her own labor and investment strategies.

Establishing a financial and legal identity involves acquiring assets (such as money and tangible items such as real estate or a car), budgeting income and expenses, establishing credit, investing, and protecting financial interests as well as legal autonomy and security. It includes education about financial and legal concepts to become a better consumer. These steps are all part of the first phase of The Confidence Continuum—*Wealth Creation*. Creating wealth isn't just something that happens—or doesn't happen. It is something you must take active steps to create.

A woman will have learned many lessons, good or bad, from her parents and peers before she reaches 18 years of age. She should also take active steps to expand her understanding of her options and select those options consistent with her goals. Courses on financial planning offered through adult education programs or community colleges are a great way to learn about investing, budgeting and establishing credit or essential legal directives. Chapter Ten includes other resources for financial and legal education on these matters.

STARTING OUT OR STARTING OVER

Here are eleven (11) things you can do to place yourself on a firm financial foundation for creating wealth when you first venture out on your own or when you start over after a divorce or other financial crisis:

1) *Determine Your Net Worth.* Sit down and add up all of your assets—everything you own, whether you are making payments on it or not. This will include your home, your car, your savings and checking accounts, your investment accounts, stocks, savings bonds and retirement accounts—everything. It will also include your personal property like home furnishings, collectibles and heirlooms. Value the property at its fair market value—the price at which you could sell it to a willing buyer. This is your asset total.

   Then add up all of your liabilities—everything you owe. Your mortgage, car, credit cards, student loans, etc. Include the total amount you owe, not just your monthly payments. This is your liability total.

   Subtract what you owe from what you own—assets minus liabilities. This is your net worth. The value of your "estate" if you will, after all debts have been paid. You should consider calculating your net worth on an annual basis to measure your progress in asset accumulation, part of your wealth creation.

2) ***Create a Budget.*** Figure out all your sources of income—your salary, social security, child support, alimony, investment income, etc. Carefully calculate all of your expenses. Start first with your fixed expenses—those that don't change much on a monthly basis such as your savings allowance (under the theory of "pay yourself first or you'll never make rooms for savings"—see step 7 below), mortgage or rent, your car payment, student loan payments, credit card payments, utilities, a reasonable food allowance and clothing allowance. Your income minus your fixed expenses gives you a number called your "discretionary income"—money that you can spend in any way you like. Allocate this income to things like entertainment, travel, etc.—the luxuries in life—things you can scale back on if needed. Then monitor your spending on a monthly basis to see how you are doing and where you can make adjustments.

3) ***Establish Credit in Your Own Name.*** It is important to have credit in your own name that is not tied to the credit history of your parents or spouse. It may also be important to hold some assets in your individual name so that there is no possibility of anyone else taking advantage of those assets for their own benefit. Having your own credit and financial accounts is a big step in establishing financial independence. It can give you flexibility if you get divorced. It can help you to establish yourself more quickly on your own again.

Limit your credit card charges to only those things you can pay off in full at the end of the month. See below how Phyllis created a method to help her do this. Don't use home equity lines of credit to finance depreciable items such as cars, boats or other items that don't improve the value of your home. Don't pledge your home, your life insurance or other critical assets as collateral for business ventures that may have an uncertain future. Don't co-sign or guarantee the debts of family members or friends for any reason.

4) *Pay All Your Bills Timely.* No matter what is happening in your life, paying your bills in a timely manner is critical. You've worked hard to establish your credit history—don't let unexpected events ruin your efforts. If possible, schedule your regularly occurring payments electronically so that they are always paid on time. This might be done through your bank's bill pay service or through automatic deduction from your checking or savings account. If you elect to do this, you'll want to balance your accounts on a monthly basis so you always know your balance. It is also a good idea to have your paycheck and other sources of income deposited electronically so that you don't have to rely on yourself or anyone else to make trips to the bank. Some creditors will even offer an interest rate reduction for payments made automatically.

5) *Establish a Credit History.* One of the best ways to establish credit is to get a credit card in your name and then use it wisely. Don't charge more than you can pay on a monthly basis and always pay your card on time. If you have difficulty getting a credit card you can consider a secured card where you post collateral, such as a savings account or Certificate of Deposit (CD), in exchange for the line of credit. These are sometimes called "passbook loans." The net effect is that your overall loan interest rate is lower because you still own the savings account balance which earns interest while you pay off the loan. When the loan is paid in full, you retain the savings balance along with the earned interest. However, if you fail to pay, the creditor has a right to take the collateral.

This means you may have to save up some money first in order to get enough collateral. Start with a low credit limit and then build up your limit as you prove your creditworthiness. After a period of time, you can try and negotiate an unsecured credit card. Credit card companies these days seem to send credit offers on a daily basis. The less you need credit, the more likely you are to receive these offers. Just use caution. Don't apply for every card that arrives in your mailbox. You only need enough to meet your emergency needs when you can't pay cash. Excessive open credit may not reflect well on your credit history, so beware.

Review your credit report regularly. Reviewing your credit report on a periodic basis is important. Credit agencies make mistakes or you may discover other items on your report that you want to explain or correct and it will be easier for you to correct these problems as you go along rather than to discover a problem when you need a clear credit record. There are three (3) major credit reporting bureaus: Equifax, 800-685-1111; Experian (formerly known as TRW), 888-397-3742; and Trans Union, 800-916-8800. You can generally obtain your report for a modest fee and if you've recently been turned down for credit, they must give you a copy for free. There are also services that you can sign up for that entitle you to periodic credit reports. Today, many credit card companies offer identity theft protection services which include periodic credit reports so you can make sure someone isn't using your credit without your authorization.

If you discover an error in your credit report, write to the credit reporting agency (keep a copy), explain the discrepancy and ask them to correct or investigate the error. There are procedures for disputing your credit report and you will want to take advantage of these.

6) *Establish an Emergency Reserve.* Establishing and regularly funding an emergency reserve is a great way to prepare for possible future financial setbacks. A good rule of thumb is to have at least six (6) months expenses saved in reserve—enough money to pay all your bills including your mortgage, car payment, food, insurance and medical expenses. A good way to accumulate your emergency reserve is to adopt the philosophy of "pay yourself first." This means the first check you write every month is to your emergency reserve account— not the one you hope to write after all the bills have been paid. If you aren't doing this now, start right away and you'll be surprised how quickly your emergency reserve will grow.

After you've established your emergency reserve, don't stop there. You may want to save for future purchases and you definitely need to save for retirement. If your employer offers a retirement plan where you can defer a portion of your income before taxes, definitely take advantage of this opportunity. The money will come out of your paycheck before you even see it and you won't miss it. But you will appreciate how it grows over time. And, if your employer matches any part of your retirement savings, try and get the full match—that's like free money as long as you remain employed. If your employer doesn't offer a retirement plan, then the responsibility is yours. Establish a Roth or Traditional IRA and commit yourself to making the maximum yearly contribution. You don't have to make the contribution at all at once. Set up a monthly automatic withdrawal to leverage the benefits of "dollar cost averaging"—an investing strategy that helps you avoid buying or selling at inopportune times and helps you to lower your overall investment costs.

7) *Make Saving a Priority.* Wealth creation begins with a solid financial foundation, not the least of which starts with saving a portion of your earned income. As mentioned, this concept is known as "paying yourself first." What this means is that when you sit down to pay your expenses each month you should write the very first check to savings—whatever that amount might be. You should strive to save at least ten percent (10%) of your income. This is hard but critical. The important concept is to simply do it, and do it regularly. The easiest way to discipline yourself to this critical routine is to have the money automatically deducted from your paycheck so that you don't even miss it. You can't spend what you don't have. If your savings comes out first, you won't even know it was there. If you wait to put something aside after you pay your monthly bills, the chances are you won't put anything into savings. It is more likely that you will find other things to spend the balance on assuming there is anything left. Where and how you invest your savings money is the next step in the wealth creation process.

8) **Get Educated.** Financial education can never hurt you. The more you learn, the better financial decisions you will make for your future. Check your local newspapers for complimentary workshops on financial topics and then take advantage of those opportunities. Your local community college or adult education center may also offer educational opportunities.

Many advisors, including the authors, spend a great deal of time speaking to local groups or conducting in-house workshops and appreciate audiences who are interested in learning as much as they can about the presented topic. Financial and legal professionals regularly conduct educational workshops or seminars for the purpose of introducing themselves to potential new clients. This is also a good way for you to "interview" possible trusted advisors without the pressure of a one-on-one consultation. See if you like their style, their personality and the advice they have to offer. Do they make the topic understandable? Are they really trying to educate you, or are they simply trying to sell something? You can learn a lot about the individuals teaching the program just by attending and asking important questions.

The National Association of Investment Clubs provides classes and has educational materials for members who are interested in investing in stocks and other financial vehicles. The membership price is modest and you can learn at your own pace. Other resources for financial education appear in Chapter Ten.

9) **Build a Strong Trusted Advisor Team.** Your advisor team should ideally consist of an estate planning/legal practitioner, a financial advisor and a certified public accountant (CPA). There may be other advisors for your team like a mortgage broker, realtor, life coach or personal trainer, but your core team should include a legal and financial advisor. Seek out individuals that you have a good rapport with. Try and find people who know each other and are willing to work as a team, not just with you independently. Interview team members to determine who will be the best fit for you. Then consult with your team on a regular basis and heed

the advice they offer. If you don't like their advice or don't trust them, then update your team. This is your team and the purpose is to provide you with the guidance, education and support you need to succeed.

If you think you can't afford to compile a professional team, think again. You can't afford not to have a team that will help you accomplish your goals. Most of us are not very good at going it alone. Professional athletes understand that coaches can bring their skills to levels beyond what they can do on their own. We all need the support and guidance of experienced professionals who can keep us on track, hold us accountable and provide the good advice that we need. Unless you are an expert in financial and legal subjects, you probably want and need the advice of a professional. Even though our background is in law and finance, we've created our own trusted advisor teams. Your team members may change over the years as your geographic location or needs change. You should feel confident that if something happens to you that your plan will be executed in the way it was designed and that your loved ones will have the professional advice and support they need to carry on without you.

10) ***Review Asset Ownership and Beneficiary Designations.*** Make sure your asset ownership and beneficiary designations are consistent with your estate and financial goals. Understand which directives control the disposition of each category of asset. Make sure your advisors bring their expertise to your asset ownership and estate planning decisions to avoid planning blind spots and conflicts. Chapter Four outlines these asset categories and the various directives that control each.

11) ***Review and Update Your Plan Regularly.*** Review your financial plan at least annually to be sure you are on track to achieve your goals and to avoid planning gaps and conflicts that may arise since the time when the plan was originally created.

Review your estate plan at least every two to three years to make sure it remains consistent with changes in your life, changes in the law, changes in your lawyer's experience and changes in your legacy.

These suggestions are just a starting point. Your financial and legal advisors can help you come up with more ideas that will provide you with financial security and help you achieve your goals on The Confidence Continuum.

INVESTMENT CONCEPTS

Risk versus Reward and Risk Tolerance: An important concept to learn is that of "risk and reward." The higher the risk a person is willing to take—in other words, their risk tolerance—the greater the potential future reward.

Gambling is a perfect example of this dynamic. There is a higher than average risk that you may lose all of your money in gambling. Therefore, the potential payoff for "investing" in this activity must be high to entice people to choose it. We've all dreamed of being the person who puts a quarter in the slot machine and wins the grand prize! In essence, consumers are saying, "You have to pay me more to put my money to that level of risk." If we are going to put something at risk, we want to be sure it will be worth it. The degree of risk we can tolerate depends on a number of factors, not the least of which is the potential reward.

In investing, a person has to gauge their own personal risk tolerance. Not everyone is going to have the same tolerance level. What one person can tolerate on the risk vs. reward spectrum, another person would find very uncomfortable. Some people don't have any problem at all investing in the stock market and others wouldn't dream of investing their money in anything other than a savings account or Certificate of Deposit. The risk-reward dynamic is one of the factors that drives the financial markets.

Correspondingly, depending on your risk tolerance, the rates of return you are able to earn on investments may be vastly different. Assume that an investment in the stock market can produce an average return of 8% over a ten year period. That sounds like a good rate of return. The catch is that this return is an average which means that the return may have been 20% one year and only 2% or even a negative percentage in other years. If you can't stand to see your investment fluctuate in value, then your investment choices become more limited.

A Certificate of Deposit (CD) allows you to lock in to a predictable rate of return and your principal won't fluctuate in value. You will discover, however, that the long term average rate of return on a CD will be much lower than an investment with a greater risk vs. reward ratio. Ask your investment advisor to help you determine your risk tolerance so that you can choose investments that are going to be consistent with your temperament, goals and time frames. However, make sure you and your advisor are using the same definitions regarding risk tolerance. It is all too common for many investors to say their tolerance for risk is high and that they can tolerate market fluctuations. These investors can have seriously anxious moments that lead to panicky sell offs due to their concerns about losing money which is some indication that their tolerance wasn't as high as they estimated after all.

Compound Interest: A woman who learns and applies the principle of investing called "compound interest" can accumulate a large sum of money with even a modest investment. The concept of compound interest is a mechanism of investing that leverages time and interest to grow a sum of money. Interest is paid on the principal balance at specified intervals (the compounding period)—daily, weekly, monthly, quarterly, or annually—and then interest is also paid on the interest previously earned—hence the compounding effect. The longer the time-line for investment, and the more frequent the compounding period for applying interest, the more interest that is earned and added to the pot until the pot doubles, triples, quadruples, and so on—like a ball of snow growing larger and larger as it rolls down a snowy hill. Albert Einstein is quoted as saying that "compound interest is the most powerful force in the universe."

To illustrate the effect of compounding and risk tolerance, let's assume that a young woman invests $2,000 at age 18—a gift from her parents or grandparents. She invests the money at a 7% rate of return. As a result of life's circumstances, she never adds another dime, but forgets about the account. At age 60, she'll have accumulated $34,288.51. That same investment at a 4% rate of return yields only $10,385.57 over the same time period. Just a three percent additional rate of return gives almost three times the investment!

If this same young woman invests the same $2,000 at age 18, but continues to add annual deposits of $2,000.00 and that amount grows at an interest rate of 7% (compounded monthly) and if she leaves it there, untouched, for 42 years she will have accumulated the sum of $547,753.62 by age 60! A woman who waits until age 40 to invest the same amount of money annually at the same rate of interest will only earn $95,405.04 by the time she reaches age 60. You can see time really makes a dramatic impact. Getting started saving at an early age, earning the highest rate of return you can and keeping it going makes all the difference.

Other Investment Principles

The American Association of Retired Persons (AARP) says there are five basic principles to guide a person in making investment choices and building a strong financial foundation for future security.

They are:
- Keep fees low
- Use index funds
- Diversify your investments
- Rebalance to stay on track
- Keep it simple

Keep Fees Low

Investment fees and expenses can reduce your net returns over time. This applies to all types of financial products, including checking and savings accounts, Certificates of Deposit, money markets, mutual funds, individual stocks and bonds, insurance and mortgages.

If you have a checking, savings account or money market account, you need to know how much the bank is charging you for this privilege each month. Many banks offer free checking and/or savings if you maintain a minimum balance or have direct deposit. However, there can be hidden fees that slowly erode your the money on deposit. Make sure you know what the true costs will be. Certificates of Deposit can have interest rate penalties for early withdrawal, even if they don't have any other costs. Debit cards may have a per use fee for withdrawals or purchases.

If you are investing in mutual funds—a diversified investment portfolio that is professionally managed—you need to know the difference between "load" and "no-load" funds. Load funds charge an up-front sales fee whenever you make an investment. No-load funds do not charge an up-front sales fee but may charge a declining sales fee if you remove your money within a specified time period. All mutual funds can have hidden charges and expenses. Be sure and consult with your financial advisor so that you understand all of the different types of fees a mutual fund may charge. Look for those with the lowest costs, called expense ratios. Visit *www.sec.gov* for more information on calculating mutual fund charges.

If you want to buy individual stocks or bonds, you will want to keep your trading expenses (the cost of buying and selling) low. Full-service stock brokers charge a hefty commission every time you buy or sell. Discount brokerage firms or on-line trading may offer more attractive fees but you'll be fully responsible for making all of your own investment choices.

Use Index Funds

Index funds are low-cost mutual funds that seek to mirror the performance of the broader stock or bond markets. Investment research shows that even professional mutual fund managers who try to buy and sell individual companies based on their own research and experience have a hard time outperforming the market indexes over time. That's why index funds are so popular.

What is an index? An index is a general indicator of price trends in a group of stocks or bonds. So, when you hear that the market went up or went down, what you are actually hearing is a report on an index. An "index fund" is a group of stocks or bonds that professional money managers believe collectively represent a larger group of stocks or bonds, such as "all small company stocks," or all "stocks on the Nasdaq," or "all high tech stocks."

Index funds are generally a mutual fund that hold all (or a representative sample) of the stocks or bonds that are included in a particular index.

The purpose of the fund is to mimic the performance of that index. If the index goes up, your fund makes money; if the index goes down, your fund loses money. There is no active management of the fund—once the group of stocks and bonds is chosen, the representative sample doesn't change unless the index is changed. Actively managed funds are those funds that employ professional money managers for their skill and expertise in selecting, buying and selling stocks and bonds with the goal of outperforming the market itself and/or indexes.

Some people like index funds because they take the guesswork out of investing. Pick the index market you like (e.g., stocks and/or bonds), and buy the index fund that corresponds with it. Index funds generally tend to have lower costs than other mutual funds because 1.) They are less complicated to manage and operate and require fewer employees; and 2.) They require less active buying and selling which means there are fewer tax consequences (losses or gains) passed on to the fund share owners. Lower costs means the net profit to share owners is higher. This means you have more dollars to invest in the fund rather than to operate the fund.

Diversify to Reduce Risk

The old saying about "not putting all of your eggs in one basket" is especially true when it comes to investing. Diversification means spreading your investments among different asset classes, such as stocks, bonds and cash equivalents. It also means having exposure to a large number of different companies so that your investment success isn't dependent on a single company or sector of the market.

Nobody can tell with certainty which investments will rise or fall in price. However, if you diversify your investments across a broad range of categories, you will reduce your overall risk and improve your chances of an increased reward for that risk. If you invest in more than one mutual fund, make sure the stocks the individual funds invest in are not too similar in terms of industry or market features. You might own 6 mutual funds but you will not have true asset diversity if they all invest in the same stocks. Make sure you diversify the types of mutual funds you select for this reason.

Rebalance to Stay on Track

Once you've made your investment choices, you may not realize that it is important to revisit those choices periodically. Investment performance can change over time, so can interest rates, as well as a person's personal risk tolerance. Rebalancing your investment portfolio periodically helps you maintain your focus and make sure your investment goals are on track. It is a lot like getting on the scale from time to time to make sure your weight remains where it should be. Once you have that "reality check" you can modify your diet accordingly. Reassessing your portfolio against the current market trends and your goals will create a reality check that helps ensure that your portfolio remains a good fit toward your goals.

For example, let's say that you've decided you want 60% of your money in stocks, 35% in bonds, and 5% in a money market fund in order to save for a comfortable retirement. This gives you plenty of potential growth (stocks), a good amount of lower-risk bonds that will produce income but balance out some of the risk in the stocks, while allowing you to keep a small portion of your money anchored in a very safe, very low-income money market fund (cash) for easier availability.

Six months later, the stock market has zoomed upward. When you check on the percentages of your holdings in each investment category, you see that your stocks have increased in price so much that now they make up 70% of your portfolio while bonds are now only 25%. Your portfolio is now "out of balance." So, happily, you sell some of the stocks; then you take those profits and buy more bonds. The goal should be to get back to 60% stocks and 35% bonds. Now you're back on track with the both the growth potential of stocks and the safety of bonds you want. If you invest in actively managed mutual funds, the money manager normally will monitor and regularly rebalance the portfolio so you don't have to. This is why such funds have management fees.

It is also important to re-evaluate investments and rebalance your portfolio if your life goals change. Things do change, and often. Your family and financial circumstances can change; your career goals, marital status and other life altering events may come along and influence your future goals and decision-making.

A time honored principle in investing is "buy low, sell high." Rebalancing your portfolio on a regular basis forces you to sell investments that have gone up in value, permitting you to capture the increased value, and to look for new opportunities elsewhere. The same might be said for rebalancing our lives on a regular basis to take advantage of new and different opportunities that may present themselves.

Keep it Simple

There are over 10,000 mutual funds in the United States and just as many choices in stocks, bonds and other investment vehicles. So which mix of investments is right for you? How do you find out? And how can you be confident that you've made the right decisions?

Having too many choices can be overwhelming, making it difficult to manage risk across different types of markets, ensure proper diversification and be confident that all of your investments are working toward your goals. Tracking the progress of your investment portfolio takes time—not to mention dedication and attention to detail—but is necessary to ensure that your investments remain a good fit for you.

Owning a few simple, well-chosen investments is a sound approach for many investors—especially if you are the type of person who can't or doesn't want to spend a lot of time tracking them. You should resist the temptation to own "the next best thing"—even in mutual funds. An investment that may be right for your best friend, may be a disaster for you. If you don't understand an investment and it doesn't fit with your risk tolerance, isn't consistent with the time-line you need and isn't consistent with your goals, then don't buy it.

DEBT MANAGEMENT

Although creating a legal and financial identity separate from your parents or from your spouse or partner involves creating a credit presence, it is as important to responsibly manage debt and understand its role in your overall financial picture and goals. We can tend to think of credit as something separate from a financial plan. However, it is an essential component of your financial plan and can enhance the progress toward your financial goals if done properly. Used wisely, credit can give you access to opportunities that help you achieve wealth independence.

Unfortunately, the opportunity to create a credit presence is readily available at a young age, starting in college, but the sophistication with which most consumers use it is lacking. It is hard to resist the invitations to open a new account that come in the mail on a daily basis. It is easy to be enticed by the opportunity to earn "rewards." These become compelling justifications to use the card and, before you know it, you use the card even though you might not have the funds to cover the card balance when the bill is due each month.

Perhaps one of the hardest disciplines consumers need to learn about credit is how to decline an offer to open an account. When was the last time you went shopping at a big box store and the clerk at the counter *didn't* ask you if you wanted to open a new credit account in order to get an additional 10% off of your purchase that day? The credit companies are banking, literally and figuratively, on the likelihood that you will say "Yes." The rationale they hope you will adopt is, "Having a card doesn't mean I have to use it. Look how much money I can save with the rewards or discounts they offer."

The unfortunate truth is that having a credit card available means you probably *will* use it—on impulse rather than on planned purchases. This means that you can easily lose track of the little but numerous ways you spend money on non-essential things. You might not be able to pay off the cards in full each month which means you will pay interest on the cost of the purchases. That 10% "savings" you got when you opened up that account is offset by the interest charges. If you are late in paying the minimum on an account, you incur late fees and perhaps other penalties, depending on your contract with the credit company.

Easy access to credit, the fact that most consumers don't understand terms such as Annual Percentage Rate (APR), or how credit scores are calculated are all ingredients for disaster. They create a recipe for financial threats to your wealth viability over time.

Jane Bryant Quinn, the financial reporter and columnist, reported in the March 14, 2005 *Newsweek* magazine that the average interest rate on rewards cards is 1% higher, after the low introductory offer expires, than the rate on standard cards. Therefore, those rewards aren't something extra; they are something you are paying for—you just didn't know it.

She also reports that credit card statistics show that more than half of the rewards card users never collect their rewards. How ironic that one of the justifications for getting a particular card isn't even used. Given the higher interest rate for such cards, the owners are definitely getting the short end of the stick.

But the biggest kicker is that so-called "fixed" interest rates on cards are not really fixed. Changes in credit contract laws and the fine print in your contract favor the credit companies. These factors permit one card company to increase the rate it charges if you are late with a payment on a different account with a different company. You can scrupulously pay the required amount to credit company A each month. But, if you also have a card with credit company B and submit a late payment to B for whatever reason, company A can charge you a higher rate, permanently. It is easy to see how a little slip can send you into a financial tumble that gets more and more serious, threatening everything you have created.

Phyllis limits her card ownership to two. She also has a good method to keep credit purchases within her budget. She writes a check to the credit company for the amount of every purchase she makes. This accomplishes several things: 1.) It gives her an immediate sense of how much she is actually spending when she uses the card. We all probably know how it doesn't seem like we are spending money when we use "plastic." 2.) It ensures that she has funds to cover the card balance every month. She doesn't mail the check she writes after each purchase, she merely enters the check in her check register and then places the check(s) in the envelope to be mailed to her credit company before the due date. Some months the company will get one check and other months it might get four or five, depending on how much she used the card. The point is that this habit has prevented her from under-estimating how much she spent via credit so she had the convenience of not having to carry cash but always paid off her cards in full each month.

Phyllis's savvy use of credit is an example of how it can serve a useful purpose toward financial goals without creating potential threats to those goals. You can implement and create similar strategies to manage your debt objectives and goals.

BEYOND CREDIT CARDS

There are many new credit "products" available in the U.S. now beyond credit cards. The legal barriers between banking institutions and financial product institutions have been relaxed due to changes in the law. These products appear to allow us to buy more with less. Interest rates can be deceiving, however. In some states, predatory lending practices have become such a threat to the financial viability of families that the state legislature has taken steps to identify what constitutes predatory lending and implement penalties for those who perpetrate it. These kinds of situations illustrate why it is important to understand the true cost of buying assets, when to use credit, and which kind of credit is most advantageous—in other words, which credit will cost the least.

For instance, "income-stated" home mortgage loans are becoming more common. These are loans that are based on the applicant's stated income level rather than on a thorough analysis of their financial status. These types of loans might seem like a great deal because they make credit more readily available to you than traditional mortgage loan standards would permit. However, the financial companies that offer "income-stated" loans apply the risk vs. reward principles similar to those discussed in the section on stocks and bonds. Their risk is greater that a certain percentage of customers will default. Therefore, the company charges higher interest rates over the life of the loans to offset the potential risks making the true cost of such a loan over 30 years much higher than a standard loan. The income-stated loan might appear to be a good deal at the time but looks can be deceiving—especially if you have a life crisis such as divorce or illness that threatens your financial balance.

This book cannot do justice to the topic of credit. Chapter Ten lists some resources for additional information on credit. However, the topic is mentioned here to remind you that it is important to have credit but it is even more important to be a good consumer and acquire and use it wisely. A complete financial plan includes establishing access to credit. A good consumer understands the true cost of that credit and the role it plays in achieving financial protections and independence on The Confidence Continuum.

DEBT CONSOLIDATION

Despite your best intentions, you may find that you still need financial assistance in the area of debt management. Don't feel all alone—more Americans today have out-of-control debt than ever before in history. A well-executed debt management plan may be the beginning of your financial recovery and health.

Be wary of debt consolidation companies, however. Debt consolidation is the process of combining smaller debts into one larger debt that can be more easily managed. Generally this will be a longer term loan at lower interest rates with a smaller monthly payment. There are a number of ways you could consider consolidating your debt. One way is to transfer a number of smaller credit card balances to one card that may be offering an incentive interest rate for a limited period of time. Or, you could transfer higher interest rate debt to a lower interest rate credit card. Another option might be a home equity loan as long as it is not so large as to possibly endanger your home in the event you can't make your payments. One advantage to a home equity loan is that you may be able to deduct all or part of the interest payments.

The debt consolidation industry is not well regulated and many companies are disguised credit companies that earn fees in indirect ways. It is better to consult with a financial planning professional such as a Certified Financial Planner (CFP) who has been trained to see debt management in the larger context of a comprehensive financial plan. Most CFPs are fee-based rather than commission based which means they are paid on an hourly or plan basis rather than by commissions on products they sell to you.

A home equity loan where you borrow against the equity in your home may be the answer to debt consolidation for some people. Home equity loans and home equity lines of credit (referred to as HELOC) have become very popular as the market values of residential properties have soared across the country. People have been "borrowing from Peter to pay Paul" or making outrageous investments in additional pieces of property. Lenders have made home equity loans very easy to obtain with little or no financial data required and have offered attractive rates as well as offers to pay all closing costs. Some financial services firms offer "income only" or "stated income" loans which are deceptively simple but can place your financial security in jeopardy very quickly. These types of loans only require the borrower to state their income without producing proof. This means that a borrower might be placed in a loan that they cannot cover— leading to default and perhaps bankruptcy. Stiffer bankruptcy laws make cleaning the slate through bankruptcy more difficult.

Home equity lines of credit might have a place in your financial plan but you should only use them very judiciously and for only very short term types of borrowing. In addition, you should be very cautious about using your home as collateral for business ventures. If the business can't afford to finance it's opportunities, you should seriously consider whether you want to risk your home.

Personal Guaranties

You should carefully evaluate any request to personally guarantee the debt of another person. This most likely will occur if your spouse, child or friend is unable to secure a loan with their own credit, and your good credit history is needed to assist them in the loan process. One well-worn caveat is that if a financial institution is having second thoughts about extending credit to this person, perhaps you should too. You've worked hard to establish your credit score, be very careful in this area.

Business owners should limit the times they personally guarantee business loan or contracts. Sometimes, it is unavoidable, but do so only with extreme caution. Also, if your spouse is not involved with your business, avoid having your spouse join in the personal guarantee of any of your business loans. A growing number of lending institutions routinely ask for spousal guarantees when they aren't really necessary. You are exposing your spouse to possible personal financial liability and perhaps exposing joint assets to future attachment if your business can't pay its debts. You might be undermining the legal protections your legal and financial advisors put in place when they helped you decide and create the legal structure for your business. Personal guarantees should never be entered into without considerable thought and input by your advisors.

Your Strong financial foundation

Life is complicated enough. Develop a strong financial foundation, with clear goals and simple investment choices. Meet with your advisors regularly to make sure your investments are properly balanced to meet those goals. Be consistent, invest regularly and reap the benefits.

Independent women should develop the habit of educating themselves on financial matters in order to have baseline essential financial competence to live successfully and to be good consumers of financial services. For our purposes, success means being able to make informed decisions. A woman may choose to live independently or share her life with others but she should still acquire basic financial skills to avoid being a victim of circumstances. For instance, a woman's ability to manage money will dictate whether she will successfully weather career or personal set backs or whether she will careen from crisis to crisis.

And, not surprisingly, financial responsibility carries over into personal relationships. In fact, The Heart/Credit Connection study by Fair Isaac & Co. in Minneapolis and compiled by Fleishman-Hillard Research, reported in the February 27, 2006 edition of **Investmentnews**, indicates that financial responsibility was more than twice as important in a potential mate than sexual compatibility! The study also revealed that financial irresponsibility was the leading cause of stress in a relationship, over infidelity and other factors.

In addition to the topics already presented, money management skills also include the ability to understand and implement basic financial principles—such as balancing a check book on a monthly basis, filing income tax returns, making decisions about savings, investments and retirement funding, just to name a few. Financial skills can also include buying a car and, perhaps, a first home. It also means establishing and managing credit, living within a budget and having basic legal directives for personal protection in the event of disability or death.

Chapter Nine provides information about selecting advisors for your financial and legal needs. Check credentials, get references and be a good consumer of financial services. There are numerous people calling themselves financial planners in the financial services arena. Make sure you understand the scope of their experience and expertise and whether their fees will be based on commissions, hourly rates, flat fees or a combination of these. Like mutual fund fees, advisor fees can reduce the net dollars you have left to invest. Make sure you understand what you are paying for so you can eliminate unnecessary charges and put more of your own money to work for you.

Creating wealth is just the first step on the Confidence Continuum, protecting it is the next frontier. ✱

chapter four

W e a l t h   P r o t e c t i o n

Wealth creation begins the journey. As we accumulate assets and work toward accomplishing our financial goals, we understandably become concerned about protecting our assets. The Confidence Continuum requires that we be mindful of another component—*Wealth Protection*. The natural reflex should be "create it, protect it." This reflex should place us in a good position to create wealth independence. Wealth protection and wealth independence are two sides of the same coin. Protections help you maintain independence. Therefore, you need to understand the financial and legal strategies that can help you protect yourself and your wealth toward the goal of independence.

FINANCIAL PROTECTION STRATEGIES

Financial protection strategies should always include the answers to the questions, "What are you trying to accomplish and what's *really* important to you?" Interestingly, the answers are usually remarkably similar. Most people want to protect their assets and income so they and their families will not be wiped out by a debilitating illness or accident resulting in permanent disability, death, or catastrophic creditor event—such as a negligent accident, bankruptcy or professional malpractice.

Liquidity Protection Planning

"Liquidity" refers to the ease with which an asset can be converted into cash without a significant loss of value or delay. Failing to factor liquidity into your decisions about your investment mix can place you in jeopardy. If your mix of assets is not sufficiently liquid, you might have to sell them at a reduced price in order to raise cash to support yourself during an emergency or if a long-term illness strikes. Or, you might not be able to complete a sale of the asset in the time frame you need to meet an emergency. Therefore, you need to make sure that a portion of your investment mix includes assets that can be converted into cash quickly. This could be cash in a savings account or money market account. The amount of the account will depend on your specific circumstances, resources and risk tolerance.

Disability Protection Planning

Protecting your income and access to healthcare becomes critical when physical disability strikes. Even if you are married or in a committed relationship, your income is going to be critical to the on-going financial security of your household. If you are single, your income is an absolute necessity. The time to plan for the possibility of disability is before it occurs. Plan A is the "life is good" plan. But we all need to be prepared to fall back on Plan B, "life has thrown a curve," just in case we are unable to work for any reason.

Permanent physical disability is best addressed with either short-term or long-term disability insurance or both, and can include long-term care insurance, Medicare and Medicaid. Chapter Eight provides a more in-depth discussion of various programs and factors you should consider when a life crisis occurs that diverts you from "Plan A"—where life is rosey and without upsets. We have inserted a reference to disability planning in this chapter as a reminder that it is an essential piece of the wealth protections every financial and legal plan must have. Wealth protections go hand-in-hand with wealth creation.

Casualty Loss and Liability Protection Planning

Property loss insurance is essential to protect what you have created. Often, however, renters fail to obtain this insurance because they think their belongings don't really add up to much. This is what Carol thought the summer after she graduated from college. She had started her first job but hadn't acquired very much beyond her clothes, second-hand furniture, kitchen utensils and audio equipment. She lost all of these things and a place to live when her apartment burned to the ground due to an electrical problem associated with the building. What was not lost in the fire was ruined due to water or smoke damage. She found out just how much it cost to replace her modest belongings. The financial wallop of having to replace all of those things put her behind the financial eight-ball for a long time. She realized too late that renter's insurance was a good value indeed.

Mortgage companies require homeowners to carry property insurance. The initial value of the policy is normally tied to the appraisal value of the home. However, many homeowners resist increasing the insurance coverage because it will increase their premiums. They might also forego coverage for some special categories of risk as a way to "save" on insurance costs. Many do this because they only look at the first of the two factors that should be considered when deciding whether specific insurance is needed:

1) What is the risk of loss to the property? In other words, how likely is a particular harm to occur?
2) What would that harm do to you if it did occur (and you did not have insurance to cover it)? In other words, would the harm wipe you out financially? Could you cover the loss out of your emergency reserve?

If the risk is low that a loss will occur or cause much harm, you might choose to "self-insure" and cover such losses out of cash reserves. However, if the impact of the harm would be great even if the likelihood of it occurring was not significant, you should look more closely at whether it makes better sense to have insurance to protect you financially and give you piece of mind.

Liability for harm caused to others can place anyone at risk for losing a significant portion of their assets if they are not adequately insured. Insurance is a relatively inexpensive way to make sure funds will be available to cover losses caused by others or ourselves. Life insurance is discussed in more depth below in the context of replacing an income-earner's or childcare provider's contributions to the household. However, liability insurance to cover catastrophic losses caused by our own negligence is important as well. For a relatively small additional policy fee, most insurance companies provide excess liability insurance coverage to customers who carry their homeowner and automobile insurance at specified levels with the same carrier. The umbrella policy will protect the owner from losses above and beyond the limits of the homeowner or car insurance, hence the nickname "umbrella" insurance. An umbrella policy can be a very cost-effective way to insulate your assets from loss.

If you want to save money on insurance premiums, consider increasing your deductible—the amount you pay before the insurance company has to pay. When choosing or comparing insurance policies, calculate how the level of deductible on a policy correlates with its premium. You can opt to own a policy with high deductibles to keep the policy premiums low. Just make sure you can cover the deductible amount from your emergency reserves.

Death Protection Planning

The death of a spouse, partner or parent of minor children can place the survivors in financial jeopardy. The loss of the decedent's income, as well as covering the costs associated with replacing their other contributions to the household, can make the difference between surviving or facing financial ruin. For example, it is common to insure the main breadwinner in a family to replace his or her income at death. However, many families overlook the cost of replacing home and childcare services of the stay-at-home parent who dies. Their contributions to the family might not be easily quantifiable but it is important to look at how these functions would be covered if that person should die.

These financial issues at death are easily addressed through adequate life insurance. You may have an employer-sponsored plan or you may have to purchase your own life insurance plan. Insurance comes in as many types and flavors as Baskin Robbins ice cream. There is inexpensive low-cost term insurance that is temporary insurance you "rent" for a period of time, or the more expensive types of insurance such as universal, variable and whole-life varieties. These terms just mean that, in addition to the insurance component, the policy might have an investment component that earns interest. The investment component might be tied to fixed or variable interest rates and its cash value can be available to you as the owner. This chapter cannot do justice to the broad topic of insurance. Your financial professional can provide you with guidance regarding the types of coverage and the amounts that would best meet your needs.

Business Owners

If you are a business owner, business interruption insurance, key man insurance or buy-sell agreements funded with life insurance may be appropriate financial vehicles for you to consider. Your primary concerns should be providing financial liquidity for both your family and your business while avoiding the potential pitfalls that may occur if a strategic member of the business should die.

Legal Protection Strategies

Estate planning is the core legal wealth protection strategy. There are many myths surrounding the need for estate planning and the protections that different legal tools and directives can provide. Most people believe that if they've done a Will, they've done all they need to do to plan for their families. There is nothing further from the truth. No estate plan is complete without a full complement of legal directives that provide for our unexpected mental disability—not as certain as death—but occurring with increasing frequency. The age group between 16-64 years has more than five times the number of disabled individuals than the over 65 age group. Disability is not a disease of an older generation—it can affect all of us.

The real problem may not be dying too soon, but living too long. The fact is we are living longer—often with the uncertainty of what our quality of life will be. Stroke, dementia and Alzheimer's disease are all on the rise. Our nursing homes have waiting lists and it seems there is an assisted living facility being constructed on every corner. The age group over 100 years is one of the fastest growing groups in our country. If we don't construct estate plans for ourselves, then what options exist? Can we rely on the protections of our state laws to provide a quality of life (or death) that will be consistent with our wants, needs, aspirations and desires? We don't think so.

Estate planning basically boils down to creating a combination of legal directives to authorize others to manage and direct your affairs when and if you are incapacitated, and at your death. Wills and trusts, healthcare proxies or surrogates and living wills, deeds and beneficiary forms are just some of the common directives that may be included in your estate plan. The number and type of directives can be complex or simple, depending on your needs, motivation, goals and budget.

The key to good estate planning is making sure your plan is complete and understanding how each directive supports or undermines your overall intentions. If your plan has gaps or conflicts, state laws will dictate what happens to you and your affairs. These laws may not be consistent with your wishes for your care and for the protection of your loved ones.

Proper estate planning can help you maintain control and independence as well as achieve your goals. To do this you need to *1)* Identify your goals for taking care of yourself and your loved ones when you are no longer available to do so—either through incapacity or death; *2)* Understand your planning options, including their costs; and *3)* Coordinate your directives to eliminate planning conflicts and gaps.

There are a number of goals legal directives can address. The most common are:

- Avoiding probate or guardianship
- Maintaining privacy
- Providing for a spouse or life partner
- Providing for minor children or grandchildren
- Providing for special needs family members in such a way that they remain eligible for public benefit programs
- Protecting assets from nursing home costs and other catastrophic illness costs
- Minimizing state and federal estate taxes

Everyone over the age of 18 should have a core set of essential legal documents in place, a baseline *legal protection package*, to authorize the people you trust to speak for you when you cannot communicate your own wishes in financial and health matters. This legal protection package should include the following:

- Durable Financial Power of Attorney (DFPOA)
- Durable Healthcare Power of Attorney (DHCPOA), also known as healthcare proxies
- Health Information Portability and Accountability Act (HIPAA) authority
- Living Will
- Preneed Guardian Declaration or nomination forms
- Anatomical Gift/Organ Donation Declaration
- Memorial Instructions regarding your burial or cremation
- Directives that dispose of your assets at your death—either a Will or Living Trust combined with proper asset ownership and beneficiary designations

So why is it important to have this type of protection? Once you attain the age of 18—the age of majority in most states—you are considered an adult and are legally able to make all of your own decisions. This is a great milestone but one that also comes with great responsibilities. Your parents can no longer legally make your decisions for you. This can be a good thing or a bad thing. It's a good thing that you can live independently and make your own decisions—right or wrong. It's a bad thing if you are unable to make your own decisions due to illness or accident—even temporarily—but have no directives authorizing others to act for you. If your parents or another person need to act on your behalf, they may be prohibited from doing so without proper legal authorization. They will not have legal access to your bank account, cannot terminate an apartment lease or even authorize a physician to perform life-saving procedures for you.

If you have a health crisis after you reach age 18 and are unable to communicate your wishes, medical personnel are not authorized to follow the instructions from your parents. This is especially true if there is a dis-agreement among family members or others about what your instructions might be. Someone would need to petition the courts for legal authority to act on your behalf. A legal protection package, that includes disability directives, will go a long way to avoid problems that might arise. Your disability directives will specify your wishes and nominate who is authorized to speak for you when you can not communicate.

Statistics show that most young people never get around to executing a legal protection package. When we are young, disability and death seem like remote possibilities. Taking care of "that legal stuff" is something that can and does, unfortunately, wait. The irony is that the two most famous cases regarding who was authorized to speak for another and what they were authorized to do involved two *young* women—Karen Ann Quinlan in the 1970's and Terry Schiavo in the mid-2000's. The national news carried the heartbreaking stories of the battles their families had with healthcare providers and the courts. Their deaths were all the more tragic because their families can never look back on their time together without looking through a veil of pain associated with deciding what to do and the implementation of a decision that wasn't their own. If these important legal directions had been created, these difficult decisions would not have been any easier, but at least the families would have the confidence that they were following their child's wishes and that they had the legal authority to act on their behalf.

The Terry Schiavo case specifically illustrated the bad outcomes that can happen when there are no legal directives in place to authorize others to act when you can't communicate your wishes. This case involved a young married woman who suffered a brain aneurysm and was brain dead during much of her late twenties to early thirties. A legal battle occurred between her parents and her husband, who was also her legal guardian, over whether she would have wanted her life artificially prolonged indefinitely. Ultimately, the courts made the decision for her and for her family. Whether this legally imposed decision is something Ms. Schiavo would have wanted will never be known because she never left any written instructions stating her intentions either way.

Protecting Yourself if Disability Strikes

We often think of disability as a physical disability, generally a disability arising from an accident. Physical disability can and does happen, but what happens if you become mentally incapacitated and are unable to make your own decisions? During a period of mental incapacity, someone must pay your bills and make financial decisions to take care of you, your family, your pets and attend to your other obligations.

In order for someone to act on your behalf, they have to have legal authorization—either given by you in the form of a disability directive or granted by the court, in the form of a guardianship. To avoid a court ordered guardianship and its attendant costs, delays and publicity, the *legal protection package* mentioned above takes on supreme importance. Below is a discussion of the legal components of creating disability protection—called Disability Directives.

Disability Directives

Disability Directives come in two essential forms: *1)* Financial Directives; and *2)* Healthcare Directives. Both are necessary to a comprehensive disability plan.

Financial Directives

A Durable Financial Power of Attorney (DFPOA) is a directive that names the individual(s) you select to manage your financial affairs including paying bills, making investments, managing real estate, applying for disability benefits and perhaps even initiating a law suit. A broadly drafted Durable Financial Power of Attorney may give your agent the ability to do anything from a financial perspective that you could do yourself.

For this reason, the person you select as your "agent" is extremely important. The person you name as your agent is a "fiduciary" in the eyes of the law with the legal duty to act for you—the principal—the creator or maker who created the power of attorney. The law requires a fiduciary to act solely on the principal's behalf and to use the *highest* degree of good faith and care when acting for the principal. The fiduciary's duty doesn't permit him to place his own interests above the principal's interests and prevents him from self-dealing with the principal's assets. There are legal penalties when someone in a fiduciary position intentionally mismanages the assets of another person.

However, intentional bad acts by an agent aren't the only way assets can be placed in jeopardy. An agent's poor decision-making or financial inexperience can place your assets at risk as well. The unintentional loss of assets does not trigger legal penalties, however, unless the agent's standard of care of the assets fell below the standard set by state law for fiduciaries.

Authorizing an agent under a DFPOA gives the same legal effect as signing a pack of blank checks and handing them over to the agent for safekeeping. That's a lot of control to give to someone and that magnitude of control should not be handed out lightly. There are some checks and balances you can put into place to provide oversight for the agent and/or to replenish the assets lost by breach of the fiduciary's duty. These are discussed in more detail later in this chapter.

A Financial Power of Attorney can be *durable* or *not durable*. It seems counter-intuitive, but unless a Financial Power of Attorney states that it is "durable," it loses its power when the principal becomes mentally incapacitated—generally the time when the power of attorney is most important. This is a legal safeguard to ensure that principals don't inadvertently give legal authority to another that can't be revoked due to the principal's mental incapacity. If a power of attorney doesn't specifically state that it is durable, it is not a *durable* power of attorney. Therefore, only a Durable Financial Power of Attorney is useful when planning for mental incapacity.

A Financial Power of Attorney can be *immediately* effective regardless of the principal's mental capacity or it can have "*springing*" language that means it is only effective in the event of the happening of a specific triggering event—such as a period of mental incapacity as evidenced by the written certification of two licensed doctors.

A Financial Power of Attorney that is effective immediately has pros and cons. On the pro side, it is available *now* for use without any legal or logistical hurdles to demonstrate why the agent needs to act on your behalf. An immediately effective Financial Power of Attorney allows your named agent to act on your behalf as soon as the document is signed. There is no delay in permitting your agent to act. Your agent does not need to prove to a financial institution or others that you are mentally incompetent and unable to communicate your wishes.

On the con side, your agent may use the power of attorney when you are still capable of making your own decisions or in a way that is not consistent with your needs. This doesn't necessarily have to be in an intentionally malicious or bad way—just something that you do not agree with. However, you are bound by the agent's acts as long as the scope of the action is authorized under the Financial Power of Attorney and is consistent with a fiduciary's duty of care.

If the negative aspects of an immediately available Financial Power of Attorney give you pause for concern, you might decide that it is better to have a *springing* Power of Attorney. The springing feature ensures that your Financial Power of Attorney doesn't become effective until you're no longer capable of making your own financial decisions. Again, there is good news and bad news associated with this springing capability. The good news is that you have increased your protection against your agent using the Financial Power of Attorney when you are still capable of making your own decisions. The bad news is that now your agent has to jump through a few hurdles in order to show that the springing or disability triggering event has occurred. The agent will need to satisfy financial institutions or individuals to whom the power of attorney is presented that you are disabled and have met the empowerment terms contained in the directive.

How do they do this? Well, they'll probably have to obtain and then present some written documentation of disability. Generally this documentation is provided in the form of a letter or letters from your doctor(s) indicating you are no longer capable of managing your own financial affairs. Your agent will be responsible for obtaining this documentation and presenting it along with the Financial Power of Attorney to demonstrate their ability to serve as your agent. You should consider and plan for the logistical realities of obtaining this documentation.

This is an example of what might happen: Your named agent goes to your bank and presents the springing Financial Power of Attorney along with a written letter from two doctors documenting your mental incapacity. The bank teller, manager or customer relations manager generally doesn't have the authority to decide whether this evidence is sufficient. They might then direct the agent to the bank's legal department which is usually not located on site and many times not even located in the same state. The legal department will then need an attorney who is familiar with your state law so they can make a determination of the validity of the document. And this will take, oh, say, what do you think—minutes, hours or days? You can generally count on the latter. Springing powers of attorney provide a measure of protection but this must be weighed against the complexity of its use.

As an alternative, you might consider creating an *immediately effective* Financial Power of Attorney and ask your lawyer if he or she will hold the Financial Power of Attorney in escrow (safekeeping) until your agent can provide proof to your lawyer that you are disabled. Again, this may take longer than you want. It's always a balancing act—complexity of the process versus protection for you. You need to decide what works best for your situation. Your lawyer should be able to provide counsel and advice to assist in making your decision.

A Financial Power of Attorney can also be *limited in scope* or very *broad and general in scope*. The primary purpose for the Durable Financial Power of Attorney is to manage financial assets and manage legal and financial circumstances. Limited Financial Powers of Attorney list only the specific categories of acts the agent can perform for the principal such as selling real estate or making tax elections. A General Financial Power of Attorney allows your agent to handle essentially all financial transactions without many limitations. General Financial Powers of Attorney are usually preferred because it is not always possible to predict the circumstances under which the power of attorney will be needed. A power of attorney can and should be custom drafted for your particular or likely needs. Boilerplate powers of attorney often fall short when it comes to describing those events for which the power of attorney will be required.

Typical acts that can be authorized under a General Financial Power of Attorney include the ability to sell or lease a home in the event it becomes necessary to raise funds for your care; the ability to prepare your income taxes; the ability to act on your behalf in a lawsuit, either to initiate the suit or settle an existing suit; and the ability to make gifts on your behalf for nursing home/Medicaid planning or estate tax planning purposes, just to name a few.

Your average off-the-shelf power of attorney form does not address all of these concerns and rarely addresses more than a narrow set of circumstances. In fact, most off-the-shelf forms err on the side of being overly conservative in terms of the scope of the agent's powers. This is intended to safeguard the principal's assets. Remember, the principal is bound by an agent's acts that are authorized under the directive.

This safeguard can backfire in some situations, however. For instance, an adult child who is the agent for an ailing parent can't transfer assets to himself due to the rules against agents self-dealing or otherwise benefiting from a principal's assets. But who else would the parent want to transfer assets to if the parent were facing catastrophic long-term care costs and wanted to exercise asset conservation strategies under Medicaid rules? Off-the-shelf power of attorney forms, even those general in scope, would fall short of meeting this parent's needs. A power of attorney that is custom drafted after careful counseling and consideration of the principal's specific circumstances can balance the principal's needs while including adequate safeguards.

One safeguard you might consider is that you can require your agent to purchase a bond. A bond is an insurance policy against loss of your assets due to your agent's acts that are not intentional theft or other specified categories of acts. The agent will have to be insurable and bonds can be expensive. However, this can provide you with an added sense of security regarding your assets—particularly if the assets are needed for your dependents as well as for you.

Alternatively, you could include instructions that your agent must obtain approval for specified transactions from an accountant, attorney, financial planner or other specified person. This, like the bond, can be a check on the agent's authority. However, this may lead to disagreements and delays. Therefore, the selection of your agent and alternates should be limited to those who have experience, good judgment and trustworthiness. Sometimes family members do not fit all three criteria and a professional must be hired in lieu of a family member. Most professionals have errors and omissions insurance that cover their professional mistakes and misdeeds—an added measure of protection for your assets.

You should always "plan for the worst and hope for the best because anything else is just wishful thinking." Lawyers are famous and sometimes derided for thinking in terms of worst-case-scenarios. However, their legal training, real world experience and case law research illustrate how things can go awry. Their legal advice and directives incorporate this perspective to avoid mishaps and place clients in the best position should a mishap or unexpected event occur.

As with insurance, these decisions require you to consider not only whether something is likely or not likely to occur, but what the consequence would be to you and the people and things you cherish if it does occur. Your best defense is to have estate planning directives that contemplate the unique and unusual.

When choosing an agent under your Financial Power of Attorney you can name one, two or more people who will be authorized to act on your behalf. They can serve as *alternate* or *dual* agents. The alternate agent identified in your Financial Power of Attorney is a "runner-up" that fills the agent role when the first agent you named is unable or unwilling to serve in that role. Dual agents must act in tandem, rather than individually, which can add a measure of safety or hassle—depending on how well they agree and coordinate their activities. Most drafters of these documents permit either alternate or dual agents to delegate actions to others. Generally, however, the delegator is ultimately responsible for the acts of the sub-agent.

Problems can arise when financial institutions or others require proof that the first named agent cannot serve or when dual agents disagree. The Financial Power of Attorney should include appropriate language to address these potential situations.

You can revoke a Financial Power of Attorney any time while you are mentally competent. However, communicating to others that you have revoked your Financial Power of Attorney can be difficult. Revoking a Financial Power of Attorney requires you to execute a written revocation and deliver it to any financial institution or third party that might have been presented with and relied on the Financial Power of Attorney. This could be challenging because you may not know where your agent may have used your Financial Power of Attorney. For this reason, you might consider including the requirement in the Financial Power of Attorney that your agent maintain a written list of any and all parties with whom the agent has done business or to whom the agent has provided a copy of the Financial Power of Attorney.

You may also have to file a copy of your Financial Power of Attorney with a county recorder's office if you want financial institutions to rely on your agent's authority regarding the sale of real estate. In this way, the financial institution or third party can inspect the public record to verify that the agent under the Financial Power of Attorney has the authority to perform the sale in question. If you have filed a Financial Power of Attorney with the recorder's office and you later want to revoke the directive, you will need to file a copy of the revocation with the recorder's office as well so third parties are on notice that the directive has been revoked.

These considerations should underscore that there is a lot of decision-making that goes into the drafting of a Financial Power of Attorney that meets an individual's specific needs and concerns. The selection of the agents and the scope of their powers are crucial to achieving your goals and managing your affairs when you are no longer able to do so.

Each state has a "default plan" when a person loses legal capacity but doesn't have these directives in place or has ineffective directives. The state's default plan is called a guardianship or conservatorship. These are discussed in more depth later in this chapter.

Healthcare Directives

Healthcare directives authorize agents, called surrogates in some jurisdictions, to make medical decisions for you when you are mentally incapacitated or unable to communicate your wishes. Healthcare directives can have different names in different jurisdictions. The generic names are "healthcare power of attorney," "healthcare proxy" or "healthcare surrogate." The directives come into play in two distinct circumstances: *1.)* End of life situations and *2.)* Routine medical care decisions.

End of Life Situations (Heroic or Life-Sustaining Medical Treatment)

The Karen Ann Quinlan story from the 1970's or the more recent Terry Schiavo story have brought end of life situations to the general public's attention. They were reported and discussed in the national and local news and, regardless of religious, political or other philosophies, almost *everyone* had or developed an opinion about how they would want matters handled if they were faced with something similar.

The directive referred to as a "Living Will" in many jurisdictions is a document created to provide written instructions stating whether you want life-sustaining treatment or procedures withheld or withdrawn if you are unable to make informed medical decisions and are in a terminal condition, have what is known as an "end stage" condition or if you are in a permanent vegetative state.

Comfort care, such as medication, can be continued if it is to reduce pain, even if your surrogate chooses not to authorize life-sustaining treatment. The Living Will also permits you to specify whether or not you want artificially or technologically supplied food and water. Intravenous food or water will be provided in most jurisdictions unless you specifically indicate you do not want them.

The Living Will names the people you want to act as your agents regarding life-sustaining decisions. The agents cannot override the instructions set forth in the Living Will but it makes sense to discuss your wishes with your potential agents to make sure they can carry out these difficult decisions for you, if necessary. You should select someone you trust, who understands your wishes regarding the termination of life and will have the emotional fortitude to carry through. A colleague says he could never choose his wife for this role because she loves him too much. Instead, he selected his sister who he says, "never liked me very much anyway."

Each state has laws that govern the formalities required for valid Living Wills. These include definitions of specific terms in addition to formalities of execution. Definitions of terms used in a Living Will are needed in order to reduce potential disputes over your intended meaning of terms. State laws standardize these definitions. One example is the use of the word "persistent vegetative state." In addition, if you want to continue all forms of life-sustaining treatment, including cardio-pulmonary resuscitation (CPR), you should clearly state your medical preferences in writing. If your agent is authorized to execute a DNR or "Do Not Resuscitate" order, you should say so, as well as have your doctor include this instruction in your medical chart. If you have particular religious or other concerns about the use of blood transfusions or other matters, you should also clearly state your instructions and preferences in this directive.

Routine Medical Care

Situations can occur when you might be unable to communicate your wishes but you don't meet the criteria for invoking a Living Will with its life-terminating implications. For instance, you might experience a stroke that temporarily makes you unable to speak or makes you mentally incapacitated. In this event, you will need someone to sign medical consent forms and authorize your medical care. The directive for this situation is often called a Durable Healthcare Power of Attorney (DHCPOA) or Healthcare Surrogate.

The purpose of this directive is to identify the agents or surrogates who are authorized to make most healthcare decisions for you when you cannot. These directives are generally not effective until you are unable to make your own medical care decisions. In other words, they are *springing* powers of attorney limited to healthcare decisions. The DHCPOA authorizes an agent to make everyday type medical care decisions like consenting to treatment or surgery, transferring your care to or from a medical facility, hiring and firing of healthcare personnel and releasing medical information and records.

You can authorize or limit the specific types of healthcare decisions your agent can make for you. For instance, you could authorize your agent to consent to surgical procedures for you but limit the agent's ability to move you to a different healthcare facility. You can include specific directions for your agents regarding healthcare decisions that invoke religious beliefs such as blood transfusions or other procedures.

Health Insurance Portability and Accountability Act (HIPAA)

A Durable Healthcare Power of Attorney has become especially important in light of the newly implemented regulations under the Health Insurance Portability and Accountability Act of 1996 (HIPAA) that became effective in April 2003. Under HIPAA, you must name a "personal representative" for the purpose of transacting business on your behalf with your health-care providers and insurers. Healthcare providers who improperly release protected health information are subject to financial penalties. Consequently, many healthcare providers are ultra cautious about releasing medical information without a duly executed HIPAA release form. This can cause logistical problems for an agent who is attempting to transact for the care of someone if the agent doesn't have access to the principal's records.

The following stories illustrate how a healthcare provider's concerns about HIPAA standards can cause problems: A client was unable to obtain a copy of her own contact lens prescription when out of town on business because she had failed to designate such an individual in advance, in writing, at her doctor's office. It didn't matter that she was giving them verbal authorization over the phone. Another client whose husband was in the hospital in a coma needed to contact her husband's insurance company to discuss his benefits eligibility. The insurance company refused to talk with her because she was not the insured. He was clearly unable to communicate on his own behalf yet she had not been properly designated as his personal representative as required by HIPAA.

There is a debate in some legal circles as to whether a separate directive is required to meet the standards required by HIPAA. You should discuss this with your legal advisor to determine whether it makes sense to prepare a separate directive to satisfy potential challenges as to whether your healthcare proxies comply with HIPAA—just to be on the safe side. The separate directive normally will be a statement authorizing the agents named in the healthcare proxies to make decisions consistent with the authority under HIPAA.

Visitation in Healthcare Facilities

Some healthcare facilities restrict visitors to immediate family when a patient is in intensive care or other circumstances where medical circumstances dictate limiting visits. "Family" is defined by most facilities as next of kin. Unmarried couples, same-sex partners or other companions will not meet this definition and will not be permitted to visit under these restrictions.

You should create a specific authorization regarding the people who will be permitted to visit you if and when visitation is restricted to next of kin. Consult with your legal advisor to decide whether this type of authorization should be incorporated in your DHCPOA or whether it should be in a separate document. If the directive is a separate document, you should make sure it complies with the same legal formalities as the DHCPOA. This directive should also specify that it is "durable" to ensure that it retains its legal authority during any period in which you have lost mental capacity.

Organ Donation

It can be a little unnerving to some people to see the organ donation form included in the healthcare proxies—forms that are used during your lifetime albeit when you are injured or ill. However, many state sanctioned healthcare proxies include a section for your instructions regarding organ donation. We presume the rationale behind this is that if a medical emergency occurs during a time when you cannot communicate your wishes and you die, the healthcare providers will need to know right away whether you intended to donate organs at death. They don't have the luxury of waiting for your agent to locate a separate document regarding organ donation. Your agent probably would not think to locate this form when they were first summoned to the healthcare facility to handle your healthcare decisions.

Many states permit you to check a box on your driver's license regarding whether you authorize donation of your organs at death. Obviously, the license is too small to permit you to outline the details of the donation. An Anatomical Gift Declaration allows you to state with specificity whether you intend to donate all of your organs or limit the donation to specified organs. In addition, you can include information regarding special requests or whether you have previously signed your intention with regard to donation with a specific medical or educational institution.

This is a very personal decision and only one that you can make. Don't be influenced by others, consider all of the implications and then make your decision known in writing.

Guardianship or Conservatorship

State laws provide mechanisms to appoint a person to be responsible for the safety and care of another person and/or that person's finances. If you don't have the proper legal directives or if they don't cover a particular situation, your loved ones might need to get a court order granting legal authority to act on your behalf, now that you are mentally incapacitated. The process of getting this authority is called a "guardianship" or "conservatorship" proceeding and is controlled by the state probate laws. This is why it is sometimes referred to as "living probate"—the probate laws apply while you are living.

Guardianship proceedings involve three factors: 1) Determination of mental incapacity; 2) Giving of authority over the ward and/or the ward's affairs; 3) Accounting to the court regarding the ward's affairs.

First, guardianship requires that the petitioner produce medical evidence of the person's mental incapacity. The statute will normally require that the level of proof required to prove that a person has lost his mental capacity must be "clear and convincing" evidence or some other appropriate level. The courts are reluctant to take away a person's autonomy. Therefore, the level of proof is sufficiently high to confine court intervention to serious situations.

Second, the court will then determine who should be appointed the guardian of the incapacitated person—the ward. The hierarchy of state-sanctioned candidates for guardians is governed by statute. You can nominate a guardian for yourself as discussed below, but the court is not bound by the nomination.

The court might divide the guardian's authority "over the person" and "over the property or estate" of the incapacitated ward. This means that a family member might be named as the guardian over the physical well-being of the ward, but an accountant or professional guardian might be named to handle the financial affairs. This is likely to occur where the court has some concern that a family member lacks sophistication or is at risk to exploit the ward or be exploited if placed in charge of the ward's finances.

Third, regular accounting reports must be given to the court to permit it to supervise the guardian's activities. Expenditures from the ward's assets must comply with specific standards and the court will review all accounts on a regular basis—usually bi-annually or annually. Failure to comply with the standards required by the court can be grounds for removal of the guardian.

The guardian can normally receive reasonable compensation for handling the ward's affairs. Non-family members who are named as guardians are usually required to secure a bond (like an insurance policy) to cover losses to the ward's financial accounts due the guardian's fault or neglect.

If the ward regains mental capacity, the ward will need to produce medical proof of this fact and convince the court to return authority to the ward to handle her own affairs.

Pre-Need Guardian Declaration Directive

A Pre-need Guardian Declaration is a directive that states your preference as to who should be guardian over your person or your property in the event your disability directives are ineffective or absent. As stated above, state statutes will generally favor family members over friends or companions unless you make your selection known. Again, the court is not bound by your nomination. However, most courts are inclined to follow a nomination unless evidence is presented to indicate that this is not an appropriate nomination.

A Pre-need Guardian Declaration is normally what we refer to as "a sweater in a suitcase." You don't need the directive at the time it is created but, like that extra sweater you pack when you take a trip where the weather can be uncertain, it sure is nice to have it if it becomes necessary. The Pre-need Guardian Declaration stands by and is not used unless and until there is a guardianship proceeding pending.

Other General Issues Regarding Disability

In the event of a disability, unmarried committed partners face a number of hurdles that may not be present for their married counterparts. Spouses always have a preference in the eyes of the law as financial guardians and healthcare surrogates. Unmarried partners must specifically designate their partner as a guardian or surrogate or risk having blood relatives selected instead.

Disability compensation application and eligibility rules favor married couples as well. A live-in friend or companion cannot make a disability claim utilizing another's earning history as is possible with a spouse and an unmarried partner is not eligible for benefits as a dependent. Therefore, it is important that a woman with a companion who relies upon her for support make specific financial plans and arrangements to address the issues that may arise in the event she becomes disabled and is unable to work.

The same is true after retirement if a woman has to enter a nursing home—the rules do not favor unmarried couples. For any type of government eligibility program, the rules for unmarried individuals are inevitably the rules that apply to single individuals. In some instances, this can be an advantage or it can be a disadvantage. If a woman lives in a "spousal support" state, marriage may actually be a disadvantage—especially if one spouse needs to qualify for Medicaid but the family assets exceed the limitations for eligibility.

Death Directives

As the old saying goes, "You can't take it with you" but it is common to hear people say, "When I win the lottery," and "If I die." The reality is few of us experience a huge financial windfall and none of us gets out of here alive. Ben Franklin may have said it best back in 1789 when he announced, "Nothing is certain in life except death and taxes." This is still true today. The difference is change. Change in when and how we are dying and change in our structure of taxation. Will Rogers may have even said it better, "The difference between death and taxes is that death doesn't get worse every time Congress meets!" Why then are we so hesitant to plan for the one thing in life that's truly certain?

In order to effectively transfer our property to our intended beneficiaries and with minimal exposure to costs such as estate taxes, we must create death directives. Death directives fall into three broad categories: Probate, operation of law and contractual rights. Therefore, it is crucial that you understand which category your assets fall into and make sure that your death directives for them are consistent with your goals.

Your *legal protection package* will normally be anchored with one or both of two directives: a Will and/or Living Trust. However, remember that you still have to coordinate them with your other directives to avoid planning gaps and conflicts.

Wills

A Will is your written expression of your last wishes regarding what should happen to your property in the event of your death. In other words, a Will is a death-planning directive. A Will is completely ineffective in the event you become disabled during your lifetime. To plan for this possibility, other legal directives—your Disability Directives—such as your Durable Financial Powers of Attorney and Durable Healthcare Powers of Attorney are essential components of your plan.

A person who makes a Will is called the testator or testatrix. A person who does not have a valid Will is said to have died intestate. Intestate succession is the term used to describe the state-imposed distribution pattern to family members and determines the next-of-kin who will inherit property when the deceased died without a valid Will.

Wills don't have to follow a particular format, but they usually do. The first paragraph normally recites the essential elements about the maker of the Will being of legal age and sound mind, and how the making of the Will was her own free act. The next paragraph in a Will normally authorizes payment of the maker's debts, the costs of administration and taxes from her estate after death. The next paragraph may direct the distribution of personal property and the following paragraph will generally direct the remainder of the estate to whomever she wants. This is normally referred to as the "residuary estate" clause because it directs the balance (the residuary) of the estate after paying taxes and debts.

Your Will should also nominate someone to act as the personal representative of the estate, called the executor (male) or executrix (female). This clause can specify whether they must post a bond and whether they are entitled to collect a fee for performing their duties as the personal representative. A bond is an insurance policy to protect the estate from losses caused by the personal representative if they fail to properly carry out their duties. The personal representative will assume the responsibility for the administration of your estate.

If minor children are involved, your Will should contain a clause nominating a guardian and alternates for your children and other provisions, such as a testamentary trust created under the Will for taking care of the children's property until they reach the age of majority or some other specified age.

Even if you own your assets in a way intended to avoid the probate process, it is a good idea to have a Will anyway. Wills can act as a safety net if there is a defect in another transfer mechanism or if you die with an unexpected asset in your own name. One way this can occur is if you receive an inheritance from a family member and die shortly thereafter. The Will controls those assets rather than requiring application of the intestate probate rules.

Living Trusts

Many people believe that a Living Trust offers "total protection" in the event of incapacity as well as death. Total protection may include protection from a forced guardianship in the event of mental incapacity, to the avoidance of probate at the time of death. Total protection may mean different things to different people. Total protection may, in reality, not offer any form of protection at all. The benefits to be derived from a Living Trust are dependent on a large number of factors including the creation or design of the trust, the drafting of the trust, the ownership of assets controlled by the trust and the actual instructions contained within or as an adjunct to the trust.

Many articles and books have been written about the advantages of having a Living Trust as the primary estate-planning tool instead of a Will. In general, the books that support Living Trusts describe the benefits of a

Living Trust in terms of the protections that may be provided in the event you become incapacitated during your lifetime. In addition, the literature advises when assets controlled by the trust are properly owned, a Living Trust can avoid probate—a dreaded result for many individuals. There can also be significant estate tax and asset protection advantages provided by proper trust planning.

The popular reasons people create Living Trusts are:

1) *Privacy.* In theory no one will know what assets are owned by your trust. A trust is a private document that is not recorded in the public records and is not required to be reflected in the records of the probate court. Therefore, privacy can be provided for you and your beneficiaries.

2) *Avoid Delay.* Theoretically, there should be no delay in the distribution of your assets from a Living Trust to your beneficiaries after your death. One potential client told us that a Living Trust could be settled in less than an hour. The reality is that the trust administration process requires several steps—steps that are similar in nature to the probate process. These steps include gathering and valuing the trust assets, making sure all creditors have been fully paid and then distributing assets to the necessary beneficiaries. This process can be short or long depending on the nature and complexity of the assets and the value of the estate.

3) *Currently Effective.* A Living Trust, unlike a Will, is effective on the day it is created. You don't have to wait for disability or death for the value of the Living Trust to become apparent. A Living Trust allows you to manage your assets while you are alive and well, while setting up the instructions necessary to provide for you in the event of incapacity or death.

4) *Amendable and Revocable.* A Living Trust is both amendable and revocable. Nothing you include in your trust today can't be modified or changed in the future. This is especially important over time as the primary elements that will change in your life are the four L's: *1)* Life, *2)* Law, *3)* Lawyer, and 4. Legacy. Each of these elements is likely to change (and on a regular and recurring basis) in your life. We will discuss these factors in greater detail later.

5) ***Disability Protection.*** If you become mentally incompetent, a Living Trust is designed so your disability successor trustee can "step into your shoes" and manage your financial affairs. This process prevents a court-administered guardianship proceeding whereby the court takes control of your financial affairs. We refer to guardianships as the worst possible kind of lawsuit—a lawsuit whereby your family files a lawsuit against you to have you declared incompetent, you get to pay for the lawsuit and you lose all of your rights to manage your life and your financial affairs.

6) ***Protection for Family Members.*** A Living Trust can incorporate instructions for the creation of additional trusts that can protect your spouse or life partner, your children, disabled family members, and yes, even your pets. These additional trusts may provide tax relief or create creditor or asset protection. They can also provide protections in the event of divorce, catastrophic illness, bankruptcy or business failures. Trusts can protect heirs from themselves in the event of drug, alcohol or chemical dependency disorders and they can protect governmental benefits for disabled persons.

7) ***Minimize Estate Taxes.*** Drafted correctly, a married couple can maximize each individual's estate tax exemption and thereby minimize overall estate taxes. When the trust is properly drafted and the assets are correctly owned, the estate tax savings may amount to hundreds of thousands of dollars.

What attributes should you look for in a Living Trust? How do you tell a good trust from a bad trust? Is the trust you have well-written and designed to meet your needs? One way to begin answering these questions is to consider the process you experienced when you created your Living Trust. How did you first learn about Living Trusts? Did you do some self-study by reading books or articles on the topic? Did you attend a seminar? A workshop? Was the purpose of the seminar or workshop to provide you with information or sell you a product? Did your legal or financial professional suggest you consider Living Trust based planning? After you made your first contact with the legal professional, how did the process proceed? Was there an educational base to the process or did you feel that your personal information was simply being entered into a word processor? Did you have an individual comprehensive design meeting that required your understanding and participation in the creation of your plan? Were the final documents fully explained to you before signing? Did you understand what you were signing and the legal effect of the document in the event of your disability or death? Were you asked to prepare any personally constructed documents to supplement your plan and provide for your well-being in the event of disability or death—documents like personal property memorandums, instructions to healthcare providers or successor trustees, or memorial instructions?

Most people we meet who have previously prepared Living Trusts have no idea what their trust was designed to accomplish. Many have put their complete faith and trust in their bank or corporate trustee, their financial professional or their legal professional without a solid understanding of the legal effect of the documents they have created.

Some people cite the cost of creating and maintaining a trust as one of the primary disadvantages of Living Trust planning. If you consider only the cost associated with having a trust drafted as its value, a trust might appear to be more costly than a Will, for instance. However, if you look at the higher level of protection that trusts can give you and your loved ones during life, during disability and at death, trusts are very cost effective.

Trusts also require education regarding asset ownership. In order for your trust to control your assets and have your trust instructions apply, you must own your assets in the name of your trust or ensure that your trust is named as the beneficiary of your life insurance, annuities, retirement plans and other beneficiary designated assets.

Trusts can be created to accomplish a variety of goals and address unique needs. You can have more than one type of trust, depending on your particular circumstances. Trusts can be "living" trusts or "testamentary" trusts. They can be revocable or irrevocable. An explanation of these terms is below.

A trust only controls property that is held in the name of the trust. The process of changing the title of assets into the name of the trust is called "funding" or asset integration. Assets held in an individual's name or as joint tenants with rights of survivorship are not controlled by the trust terms.

As mentioned, a Living Trusts become effective when it is signed—while you—the trustmaker—is living. Living Trusts are also called *inter vivos* trusts, which is the Latin term meaning "between the living." The provisions in a Living Trust can include instructions and legal authority for taking care of you and your loved ones during your lifetime, either while you are alive and well, or in the event of your disability, as well as providing for your beneficiaries at your death.

Testamentary trusts are trusts that are created in a Will. They do not exist (except on paper) until the maker of the Will dies and the Will is administered through probate. Therefore, unlike Living Trusts, testamentary trusts must go through the probate process. Because a testamentary trust does not come into existence until the maker of the Will dies and the Will that created the testamentary trust is probated, a testamentary trust cannot provide instructions to take care of the maker or her loved ones during a period of disability in the maker's life. As mentioned, Wills do not provide any disability protection during an individual's lifetime.

Living Trusts and testamentary trusts can be modified or amended anytime up to the time the maker dies or becomes incompetent. In a Living Trust, the trustmaker can authorize others to modify the trust terms even when the trustmaker is incompetent or has died. The agent in the trust who is authorized to make these changes is generally referred to as a "trust protector." A trust protector can provide significant value if the law has changed and the trustmaker is prevented from taking advantage of that change.

A trust can also be irrevocable. Irrevocable trusts are created during the trustmaker's lifetime but they generally cannot be amended after creation, except by a court order or under the direction of a trust protector, and with limitations. Irrevocable trusts are often used for gifting purposes and to remove assets from a person's taxable estate.

There are many benefits of trusts:

- Trust terms are private since they do not require probate—a public process.
- They can include provisions for disability determination and provide explicit legal authority to take care of the trustmaker and other loved ones even when the trustmaker is incapacitated.

- Assets generally are not placed directly into the name of the benefici-ary, thereby protecting the asset from being vulnerable to the beneficiary's creditors or to waste caused by the beneficiary.

- A trust can hold assets for the use of a surviving spouse or loved one during the individual's lifetime, with the balance of the assets pass-ing to others (perhaps children from a prior relationship) at the survivor's death.

- Gift tax implications will not be triggered on the trust assets as long as the assets are not transferred into the name of the beneficiary.

- The interests of children from prior relationships or other family members will be protected because assets will not transfer outright to a surviving spouse or partner.

- Trust terms can be drafted to enhance the likelihood that payments from the trust supplement rather than supplant a beneficiary's needs-based public disability benefits, if any.

- If properly drafted, trusts can provide a way to manage assets while the survivor is coping with the grieving process.

- Unlike a Will, the mechanisms for contesting a trust are more difficult than for Wills.

Trusts provide powerful planning opportunities. A trust can permit the trustmaker to dodge and weave around many of the disadvantages of other forms of disability and death planning directives.

Personal Representatives and Successor Trustees

Regardless of whether you choose a Will or a Living Trust as your pri-mary planning tool, you can't avoid the issue of personal representatives also known as executors and/or successor trustees. A personal representa-tive or executor is the individual, individuals or company responsible for carrying out the responsibilities of administering your Will when you die. A successor trustee is the individual, individuals or company responsible for carrying out the responsibilities of administering your trust when you become mentally incapacitated or die.

The selection of these individuals or companies can add to the success or failure of any estate plan. Many people select family members because of a perception that it will cost less to have an individual responsible for these duties. This may be true in some instances but can also be misguided if family members are not qualified, don't take their responsibilities seriously, mismanage estate or trust assets or promote (rather than discourage) family harmony. These people are placed in the highest position of trust imaginable. They have to be able to "step into your shoes" and make decisions that are consistent with the decisions you would make if you were available to make them personally. They can only do this successfully if they are first, qualified to handle the responsibility and second, they are given comprehensive instructions that clearly outline their rights, responsibilities and duties.

PASSING ON YOUR 'STUFF'

When we die, the "stuff" we own gets passed on to our survivors. The generic term for this process is "estate settlement" or "estate administration." When an estate is settled, title to your "stuff" is transferred to others in basically three ways:

1) Probate and Estate Administration
2) Operation of law
3) Contractual Property Rights

The method of transfer and the consequences of the transfer depend on a number of factors. These factors include:

• How title to assets is held
• What legal directives are in place to direct the assets at death
• The total value of the deceased person's estate

An effective estate plan will coordinate all of these factors with your specific needs and goals.

Title Controls

How title to assets is held and how title affects transfers of assets is one of the most misunderstood areas for non-lawyers facing estate planning decisions. Most people think of estate planning as creating a Will or a Living Trust. Few people realize that every time they open a bank or brokerage account, complete a beneficiary designation form or execute a deed, they are engaging in estate planning, of sorts. They don't realize that a Will or a Living Trust is useless if they own title to property as joint tenants with rights of survivorship (JTROS or JTWROS) with another person.

A lot of estate planning involves creating a combination of types of ownership to accomplish your estate planning goals. Consequently, it is important to understand the different categories of title, and that each specific category of title controls which mechanism is used to transfer assets at death. Without this understanding, you might not have the proper scope of legal directives to achieve your goals. Your estate planning goals can be anything from minimizing the delay and expense of administration or estate taxes to avoiding probate or providing asset protection for survivors, among a number of other worthy estate planning objectives.

The basic rules regarding how assets are transferred are the same for both married and unmarried couples. It is just that state laws build in safety nets for married partners and their children to make sure they are not disinherited accidentally. Unmarried partners have no automatic safety nets. It is essential that unmarried partners create their own safety nets to ensure that their wishes will be followed.

Understanding the rules that control transfers at death is easiest if you remember that each category of ownership has an "instruction sheet" for the disposition of the asset. The instruction sheet might be a Will, a Living Trust, a beneficiary designation or contract terms.

Probate and Estate Administration

Every estate has to be administered when someone dies. The process can be formal (probate administration) or informal (trust administration, beneficiary designation or operation of law). Regardless of its form, estate administration is essentially three distinct steps:

1) Identifying, gathering and valuing all of the assets of the decedent;
2) Identifying and paying all of the decedent's creditors and expenses of administration; and
3) Distributing the balance of the estate to the beneficiaries.

Probate is a state-authorized court process to settle the deceased person's final debts and to formally pass legal title to property from the deceased person's name to others. The probate process *only* controls property in a person's individual name. The probate process does not control property that is held as joint tenants with survivorship rights, property that passes with beneficiary designations or property that has been titled in the name of a trust. However, if there is a flaw in any of these ownership categories, the probate process might be required to pass title of the asset because the original "instructions" for that asset can no longer be followed. It is also important to note that joint title forms of ownership that do not include appropriate survivorship language (such as tenants in common) are also controlled by the probate process. If there is no Will, or if it is invalid for some reason, the probate process will follow the probate law rules for people who have died without a Will or *intestate*. Either way—with a Will or without—the system for distributing assets is called probate.

The probate or administration process is essentially the "proving of your Will" to make sure that there is a court administered procedure for ensuring that your wishes are carried out.

The term "probate estate" refers to the assets that are controlled by the probate process. The probate estate will not include property that does not require the probate process to pass title to others. Be sure to note however, the probate estate is not the same thing as the taxable estate for estate tax purposes, a concept we will discuss later.

Some of the disadvantages of probate you should consider in your decision-making are as follows:

- Probate is a public proceeding. This means the nature and extent of the probate assets can be scrutinized by anyone who cares to look up the record.
- The probate process requires filing fees, legal costs, appraiser fees for real estate and special types of assets and accounting fees. These fees can add up to sizeable amounts. (Note: some or most of these fees may be required even if probate is avoided.)
- If a testamentary trust is created in the Will, there may be additional costs to the estate for the ongoing administration of these trusts pursuant to the instructions in the Will.
- The probate process can be lengthy, depending on the nature of the probate assets. Beneficiaries under the Will generally do not gain access to the assets while the process is pending. However, most probate laws give surviving spouses access to limited sums to live on during the administration process. There is currently no comparable provision for unmarried partners to receive a similar allowance while the probate is pending. Unmarried partners are treated no differently than single beneficiaries in the eyes of the law.
- Disgruntled heirs (blood relatives) can challenge a Will before the probate judge and, perhaps, change some of the distributions set forth in the Will.

The probate process has some advantages. One advantage is that the decedent's creditors have to present their claims to the decedent's estate within specified time frames or forego payment. Another advantage is, ironically, one of its disadvantages—the fact that the process is public. This means that it is subject to scrutiny by others, a fact that may make it more difficult for mishandling of the probate estate assets. Finally, it is a court-supervised process that must follow procedures that can impose a degree of orderliness and predictability to the process.

If you've created a Living Trust and effectively avoided the probate process, you haven't avoided the estate administration process. The same three (3) steps outlined above for probate administration also apply to trusts. The primary difference is that trust administration is essentially a private administration that avoids the scrutiny of the court system. The process can be just as lengthy and just as time consuming, depending on the circumstances.

Operation of Law

States can create categories of property ownership that, by the terms of the state law, automatically give ownership of the property to the surviving owners at the death of an owner. These types of ownership are either created by the common law of a state or are codified by state statute. For example, tenancy by the entirety (TBE) is a type of survivorship ownership that is limited to married couples. Probate is not required to determine who receives the property at the owner's death.

Assets Held Jointly with Others

People can own assets with others tenants by the entirety (TBE), as tenants in common (TC or TIC) and as joint tenants with rights of survivorship (JTROS or JTWROS). Most unmarried people prefer the JTROS form of ownership but sometimes make a mistake, and do not include the required "survivorship" language when executing a deed. Therefore, they think they have JTROS when they actually have created TC ownership. The difference determines whether they need probate to pass title at death, among other things.

Tenants in Common (TC or TIC)

At death, a person's interest in TC assets is controlled by a person's Will since they own a specified percentage of the asset and can convey that interest to others during life and at death. The beneficiary(ies) under the Will becomes the joint owner of the asset with the other joint owners. There is no built-in survivorship language in a TC owned asset.

Joint Tenants with Rights of Survivorship (JTROS or JTWROS)

This form of property ownership is probably one of the most common examples of the operation of law principles. It is popular because it is easy to create and inexpensive. Many people choose this type of ownership because it avoids probate and appears to create a fair division of assets between couples, married or not. However, these so-called advantages can obscure some of the less desirable qualities of JTROS, such as:

- The asset is available to the creditors of both joint owners. Joint ownership with rights of survivorship property is subject to the creditors of either owner. If one of the joint owners has liabilities from a serious accident, a failed business or for some other reason, the jointly held property could be attached to cover the joint owner's debts. This is one of the primary reasons joint ownership of property is not recommended for even married individuals.

- A taxable gift can be triggered if unmarried owners contribute unequal amounts to the cost of acquiring the asset. When two people buy property and creates a JTROS form of ownership deed, in the eyes of the Internal Revenue Service (IRS) there is a gift to any owner who did not contribute equally toward the cost of acquiring the property. This same concept applies if a portion of the asset is transferred to a non-contributing owner after the asset is acquired.

- For married couples, this gift is not a taxable event due to the ability for spouses to make unlimited gifts to each other. For unmarried couples, unintended gift taxes can be triggered. If the portion of the property titled to the non-contributing partner exceeds the annual gift exclusion limit of $12,000, there will be an obligation on the donor/owner to file a gift tax return and report the gift to the IRS. The effect of these lifetime gifts in excess of the annual exclusion limit is to reduce the amount a person can leave at the time of death without an estate tax obligation.

- The entire value of the asset will be included in the estate (for purposes of calculating the federal gross estate tax) of the first owner to die unless the survivor can produce proof of his or her contributions to the property or other proof as to why less than the full amount should be included. The survivor might want to show less than full ownership by the deceased owner in order to reduce the federal estate tax and state estate tax, if any.

Structuring financial accounts as JTROS makes the account available to all joint owners and any owner can legally withdraw all of the account funds without the permission of the other owners. Indeed, one of the first instructions divorce attorneys normally give their clients is to immediately remove all assets from joint accounts in order to obtain control over the funds and have the upper hand in negotiations thereafter. For unmarried individuals, joint ownership with rights of survivorship may not be prudent.

There can be income tax consequences to unmarried persons who own property as joint tenants with rights of survivorship. The income tax consequences involve capital gains on property. The cost to acquire a piece of property or an asset is called the "basis." If property is later sold or transferred, the capital gain (or loss) is calculated on the difference between the basis and the sale price or its fair market value on the date of transfer. When a property transfers at the death of the owner, the tax basis of the property is the fair market value of the property on the date-of-death even if the transfer is actually finalized later. In tax terminology, this is called a "step-up in basis" which means that the recipient of the property acquires a basis in the property equal to the fair market value of the property on the date of the owner's death. Then, when the property is sold, the capital gain is the difference between the value on the date-of-death and the amount for which the property was sold. The recipient isn't required to use the value of the property when the property owner originally acquired the property. Obviously, this can save large sums of money in capital gains taxes.

The most recent federal estate tax laws have modified the rules on step-up in basis at death, and there is some debate whether these rules will remain in place. Therefore, it will be important to consult with appropriate advisors if your assets are sizeable to be sure you understand the tax consequences of transferring your estate at death.

Joint owners who receive property as a result of rights of survivorship only receive a percentage of the step-up in basis. This percentage correlates with the percentage of each individual's contribution to acquire the property.

Married couples are presumed to have contributed 50% each. However, one hundred percent (100%) of joint property will be included in the estate of the first of unmarried partners to die unless the partners can show the actual percentage they contributed to acquire the property.

Other issues to consider with regard to joint ownership:

- A joint owner requires consent of the other owner to sell real property held as JTROS during life (this can be a good thing as well—read the section on disadvantages for contract assets below).
- There is no mechanism to hold JTROS property in trust for the benefit of a disabled surviving joint owner. If the survivor is in a nursing home at the time the other owner passes away, the value of the property might make the survivor ineligible for public benefits based on financial need.
- JTROS does not work well in the event of the simultaneous deaths of owners since the property will be included in the estate of both owners. The second owner will not have time to make alternative plans. In Florida, the law presumes that if all of the joint tenants with right of survivorship die simultaneously, or it is impossible to determine the order of death, each individual is deemed to have owned 50% of the property in their individual name. As a result, the property will thereafter be distributed pursuant to the deceased's Will or state laws of intestacy.
- Federal and state estate taxes might be due at the death of the first owner and the estate might not have sufficient liquid assets to cover them. In addition to gift and estate tax consequences, if an owner, either married or unmarried, is not a U.S. citizen the rules for gift and inheritance taxes may vary. In some states, there may also be a state inheritance or estate tax at the time of death.

"He who lives last, controls." Or, put another way, "He who lives the longest wins." In any event, the surviving owner can decide who gets the asset once it is transferred to the survivor's name on the death of the first owner—regardless of the original understanding of the joint owners. Therefore, there is no guarantee the property will go to the people originally agreed upon between the owners.

This can hold particular importance to owners who want to provide for children from prior relationships after the demise of the second owner or where there are concerns that the survivor-joint owner might remarry in the future or be vulnerable to exploitation in subsequent relationships.

We have both seen examples where parents in a second relationship have assured their respective children from prior relationships that they will be provided for in the event of their parents' death. In one case, however, at the husband's death, it was discovered that the bulk of the assets were owned as joint tenants with rights of survivorship with the wife, or the wife was named as the beneficiary of life insurance and retirement plans. As a result, the wife became the sole owner of 100% of the property and she was free to use this property during her lifetime and then to distribute it at the time of her death as she might choose. She has made it clear to her husband's children that they are not included in her estate plan. This is an all too common scenario that is repeated daily upon the death of a spouse in a second or more marriage situation.

Transfer on Death Deeds (TOD) or Deeds with a Retained Life Estate or Remainder

These deeds to real estate are individually owned titles with a survivorship or remainder feature. The asset remains in the individual name of the owner but it is not controlled by a Will or the probate process because the deed has a built-in survivorship provision that directs who gets the property at the owner's death.

This type of deed is easy to create and inexpensive. The survivor merely produces proof of the death of the owner, and an affidavit is generally filed with the county recorder's office to create a paper trail showing how and why title was transferred.

TOD assets do not have all of the disadvantages that JTROS property have in terms of potential gift tax issues or being subject to a joint owner's control or creditor's control. However, some disadvantages of TOD are as follows:

- The entire value of the asset is included in the deceased owner's gross estate for purposes of calculating the federal and state estate tax.

- If estate taxes are due at the death of the owner, the estate might not have sufficient liquid assets to pay them. This may force the sale of the property to pay for the taxes.
- The asset is available to the owner's creditors during life (but not available to the survivor's creditors until the survivor receives the property in his or her own name at the death of the owner.)
- There is no mechanism to hold the asset for the benefit of a disabled survivor.
- The survivor decides who gets the asset once it is transferred to the survivor's name regardless of what the original owner and the survivor had discussed prior to the original owner's death.
- They are not available in every state.

Contractual Property Rights

Many of us have contracts that entitle us to direct the contract benefits to survivors at our deaths. Some of these contracts are associated with employee benefits at work. The most common examples of assets transferring via contract are insurance policies, retirement accounts, annuities and payable-on-death (POD) accounts.

POD provisions might appear to be the same as transfer-on-death deeds. They are not technically the same since they do not get their legal standing from state law but get it from internal policies offered by financial institutions. Therefore, they belong in the family of assets that transfer via contractual provisions rather than by operation of law.

Trusts are technically part of this category, but have been discussed separately because of their unique features. They can be drafted to overcome many of the disadvantages of other forms of ownership and also provide disability planning opportunities.

The terms of the contract permit the owner to identify who receives the property under the contract when the owner dies. The owner must complete a beneficiary designation form identifying the beneficiary. The beneficiary designation form is the instruction sheet for the proceeds controlled by the contract.

A will has no power over the contract proceeds and will not direct who gets the benefits under the contract. The only exception to this rule is if the beneficiary designation form is defective for some reason or if the named beneficiary(ies) dies before the owner dies and there is no one else named to take the benefit under the contract, or if the owner names their estate as the beneficiary. In this case, the contract will have an owner (who is deceased) but no named beneficiary. Therefore, probate will be needed to direct who gets the benefit.

We have seen disputes arise over the failure to rename beneficiaries when people have entered into new relationships. Generally, the discovery is made that someone from a long ago relationship is still the named beneficiary on the retirement plan or insurance contract. The intended beneficiary is unhappy about the prospect of not receiving the assets and inevitably brings a lawsuit to try and establish their rights. Our experience has been that most of the time the named beneficiary named on the contract prevails.

Contract assets have some of the advantages of the other ownership methods discussed above:

- There is no need for probate unless there is a problem with the beneficiary designation.
- There are no costs associated with creating the beneficiary designation.
- The transfer process is private and is not part of a court record.
- Some benefits are not considered income to the beneficiary so no income tax is due upon receipt.
- A trust can be named as a beneficiary to avoid issues associated with outright distributions.

Some disadvantages of contract assets include:

- The asset is available to the owner's creditors during life and may have been expended by the time of the owner's death.
- The asset can be included in the deceased owner's estate for purposes of calculating the federal and state gross taxable estate.

- There is no mechanism for holding the asset for the survivor's benefit if the survivor is disabled at the time of the transfer.
- If a non-spouse is the named beneficiary, the payout schedule for retirement benefits may be less favorable. Generally, a spouse-beneficiary is afforded the opportunity to roll-over a retirement account into his or her name and to continue the income tax deferral during the balance of their lifetime and potentially for the lifetime of their named beneficiaries. The ability to continue this income tax deferral is not available to non-spouses.
- An unmarried owner can change the beneficiary any time prior to death or incapacity without the consent of the beneficiary, whereas married couples generally cannot change the beneficiary from the spouse without the spouse's written consent.

A vivid example of how failure to plan and failure to update beneficiary forms can cause emotional and financial hardship for a family is the following case. An unmarried couple failed to properly designate each other on their respective life insurance beneficiary forms. They also failed to do any planning at all, and did not even have a Will to protect each other. When one of the individuals died, it was discovered that his father, not his fiance, was the beneficiary on the life insurance policy. Sadly, the father predeceased his son. Therefore, the default language in the son's insurance contract provided that his estate—not his fiance—was the beneficiary when a named beneficiary had already died.

The deceased did not have a Will, so the laws of intestacy (as determined by state law) controlled the disposition of the insurance proceeds. Under the rules of intestate succession his mother was the beneficiary of his entire estate. Unfortunately at the time, his mother was living in a nursing home, was receiving Medicaid and was mentally incapacitated. Her incapacity required the appointment of a guardian to handle the insurance proceeds. It was also necessary to implement a plan to protect her from becoming ineligible for her Medicaid benefits due to the receipt of the insurance proceeds. That's the good news.

The bad news is the surviving girlfriend brought several lawsuits to establish her rights in the home she shared with the decedent (owned by the decedent), the vehicles (owned by the decedent), the life insurance (now paid to his estate) and his retirement plan. All of the litigation, the pain, the family trauma—all of it—could have been avoided had the couple taken the time to meet with an estate planning professional, prepare the proper estate planning directives and examine the ownership of assets and beneficiary designations affecting their assets.

Legal Formalities

State laws require that financial and healthcare directives be executed with certain legal formalities. The formalities can differ from state to state and can vary depending on the specific directive in question. These directives must be created by someone with legal competence, who is of legal age and who is not executing them under circumstances of duress or fraud. Generally, the law will require that the documents be signed before a notary and/or before two disinterested witnesses who are present when you sign your name. Failure to execute a document property may render it invalid.

Some categories of people are generally ineligible to be witnesses to these directives—anyone who is related to you by blood, marriage or adoption; your attorney-in-fact (someone with a Financial Power of Attorney); and your doctor or the administrator of any nursing home in which you are receiving care.

If you are have more than one place of residence or you regularly travel to other states for business or pleasure, it is advisable that you make sure your directives comply with the standards of that state as well as your home state. Although the full faith and credit principles of the United States Constitution should permit a document properly drafted in your home state to be honored in other states, it makes sense to reduce the chance that a financial institution or healthcare provider could challenge the legality of a directive based on a technicality.

Amendments to or alterations on the directives themselves must be executed with proper formalities as well. Changes that are not within prescribed rules cannot be enforced and could even bring the validity of the entire directive into question.

Wills and Living Trusts must also be executed with certain legal formalities to be considered valid. Each state decides what formalities must be followed. In general, most states require that the maker of a Will or Living Trust have legal capacity (be competent), be of legal age (at least eighteen years old), and that the document was executed of the maker's free and intentional act. Some states may also required additional execution protections in the form of what's known as a "self-proving affidavit." You must follow the rules of the state in which you reside at the time your Will or Living Trust is executed. Be sure you understand the requirements and complexities of your state law.

Most states require that the will be written and signed by the maker of the will before one or more witnesses. Handwritten wills, called holographic wills, are permitted in many states and may not need to be witnessed but must meet other standards to be considered valid. Each state will have its own requirements for a holographic will to be considered valid. We know of one instance where a Will that was written on a piece of notebook paper in the hospital and properly witnessed was validly admitted for probate purposes. We don't generally, however, recommend do-it-yourself wills.

OTHER PROTECTION PLANNING ISSUES

Additional methods of financial and legal protection planning in the event you plan to join your life with another person—either formally by marriage or less formally in a committed personal or business relationship include prenuptial agreements, Life Alliance™ or cohabitation agreements and business succession agreements.

"I Do"—It's Not That Simple

If this is a first marriage for both parties, a prenuptial agreement, also known as a premarital or antenuptial agreement, may be the furthest thing from your mind. Many people think these agreements are only useful for the wealthy or pessimistic. Marriage is a joining of two lives. By design, or default, the couple will join financial lives as well. They might opt to keep some matters in their individual names but the consequences of marriage naturally combine resources on most levels. In light of current divorce statistics showing that approximately half of all marriages fail, every couple should at least consider whether a prenuptial is a prudent step to ensure financial security if the marriage fails. It is a prudent precaution to consider rather than reject out of hand.

Couples shouldn't disregard the concept of a prenuptial agreement completely before understanding why and when prenuptial agreements are recommended. They should compare their financial situations, prospective earning powers and possible inheritances. They should consider whether their families are similarly situated financially or whether there is a disparity in economic upbringing. If one of them supported the other through professional school or postponed career plans or education to stay home to raise a family, they should consider how to fairly treat the contributions and compromises made by the supporter/stay-at-home spouse if the marriage should fail.

These kinds of questions are just some that should be posed to determine whether a prenuptial agreement is appropriate before walking down the aisle. Being an ostrich about these kinds of issues before a marriage doesn't make sense and can jeopardize the individual security of both individuals.

Prenuptial Agreements

A prenuptial agreement is a contract entered into by an engaged couple prior to the wedding. It sets forth the terms and conditions under which the property the couple brings to the marriage and acquires during the marriage will be distributed in the event of a termination of the marriage—either by death or divorce. Many people think a prenuptial agreement is for divorce planning only. This is not necessarily true because your spouse could become disabled or die and a prenuptial agreement generally addresses a number of issues that are important in that respect. Many states have automatic inheritance rights for spouses that may be inconsistent with a couples desire to keep their assets separate.

A prenuptial agreement can reduce the disproportionate role emotion plays in the division of assets and other issues during a divorce. Often, emotion fuels battles between divorcing spouses beyond reason and prudence. The couple remains locked in a self-destructive death dance that can threaten to undermine their overall financial security. The court will rarely deliver the couple's version of fairness. It is better to discuss division of assets when the relationship is not rife with acrimonious resentments and grudges. A pre-need discussion of these issues is likely to be more fair and will ultimately be more cost-effective in the long run. In addition, the couple will be in a better emotional position to move on after the end of the marriage.

Prenuptial agreements should not be a "do it yourself" matter. There are too many details that must be considered to ensure that the agreement is comprehensive, meets legal formalities and is enforceable. For instance, if the validity of a prenuptial is ever challenged in court, most courts will look at whether there was 1.) "ink on the wedding dress"—meaning the agreement was signed too close to the wedding ceremony to permit the parties adequate time to consult with advisors and consider their options, 2.) full disclosure of assets and liabilities, and 3.) unequal bargaining positions of the parties. Agreements that were executed where one party was under duress (such as on the eve of the ceremony), or without full disclosure, or when there was disparate sophistication or unequal bargaining positions are less likely to be enforceable in part or whole—clearly defeating the purpose of the agreement.

It is prudent to insist on full disclosure of assets *and* liabilities even though it is not required in all states. Disclosure removes arguments that a party to the agreement was not aware of the assets to which they were giving up their rights.

In broad terms, a prenuptial agreement will describe the assets and liabilities that each of the parties is bringing to the relationship. This is partly done for full disclosure purposes and partly to create an adequate paper-trail to identify each of the individual party's assets if necessary down the road. Disclosing the assets is one of the most important aspects and shouldn't be taken lightly. It will also force the couple to sit down, get organized and take stock of where their assets really are. When you look at the total, you may realize that you are bringing more to the relationship than you realized and will be happy for the protection you are getting.

The prenuptial agreement should also state whether and what each party is bringing as their separate property to the marriage and whether it is intended to remain the separate property of that person during the marriage. In addition, if an asset grows in value or is exchanged for another asset, that asset will likewise be protected.

The agreement should also address how income earned during the marriage is to be handled. Will income be shared or will the individual income of party be presumed to belong to that party? In the event of divorce, will there be additional or other treatment for income and its profits earned during the marriage? These questions and their answers will be very important if and when a marriage ends, particularly if one party is not the primary income earner.

The financial details of the relationship, of course, lead to the topic of alimony. If one party is earning all or most of the income and the relationship is later dissolved, should the earning party be required to pay, in the form of alimony, a monthly or other regular payment to the non-earning party? This is a difficult question and one that should be thoroughly considered with legal counsel. Waiving the right to alimony can be waiving a significant right and you should have all of the facts.

Marge was a 63 year old widow of a Fortune 500 executive who had left her financially secure. Marge did not have to worry about her financial future. She could travel and shop to her heart's content.

Marge began dating her husband's long time friend, Bob, a few years after Bob's wife died. They had similar backgrounds and had always shared the same interests. Now they also shared the pain of losing a spouse. Bob was retired and the two enjoyed traveling and visiting Marge's children and grandchildren. They grew close and eventually married.

After six years it was clear that the marriage was in trouble. Bob did not agree with Marge's spending and generous gifts to her children, grandchildren and friends. Marge was annoyed that he spent the entire day watching sports and rarely ventured from the couch. His drinking became a source of friction for Marge. Eventually she decided she wanted a divorce.

Marge was in shock when Bob sought alimony from her. She assumed they would each leave the marriage with what they brought to it and not seek anything more. Unfortunately for Marge, she ended up having to pay a very large lump sum of money to Bob to resolve the divorce litigation on top of her legal costs. The sums paid to Bob were large enough to reduce the amount she had planned on using to help her grandchildren with college costs. But it was either that or continue to pay attorney fees to litigate the matter in court.

Marge's situation is a classic example of how assumptions can be expensive and when, how and why prenuptial agreements are useful tools for wealth protection. This is sometimes called "bloodline protection" in estate planning circles because a person's wealth is kept in the family bloodline rather than passed to others through divorce or poor judgment and inexperience. It may not be romantic to think about money when you are in love but, as stated previously, a marital relationship is a joining of financial matters as well as hearts. Therefore, it is important to give some thought to "what if" scenarios should the relationship falter.

Prenuptial agreements aren't just for wealthy widows—they are designed to provide financial protections for an uncertain future. Young couples and couples remarrying for a second or more time may also consider the benefits of a prenuptial agreement. But, it is always important to understand what is being protected or waived.

A young, twenty-something couple, Steve and Annette, had roughly similar financial assets. They consulted a colleague about a prenuptial agreement prior to their marriage—the first marriage for both. The primary concern was one raised by Steve's family because there was the possibility that some family money could be coming to him in the future when his grandmother died.

Annette was more than willing to waive any rights she might have in this potential inheritance. She was also willing to waive her right to alimony although her attorney recommended against it. The attorney's recommendation was based on the understanding that although she was currently employed and making a good living, this might not always be the case. The couple had discussed the possibility of having children and the expectation was that Annette would stay home to raise them.

Annette's attorney had legitimate concerns that Annette would be interrupting her career for a number of years to raise children. Should she find herself in the statistical majority facing divorce later on, she might not be immediately employable and may need either temporary support, a lump sum distribution or long-term alimony to help get her back on her feet and remain financially viable. It is common for couples to discount or overlook the economic price the stay-at-home spouse pays in terms of interrupting a career and keeping skills current. Women like Annette place their financial security in jeopardy if the marriage ends and they are on their own again after an absence from the work world. Consequently, waiving rights to support and other assets is something they should only do after full financial analysis by a financial professional and legal consultation with a lawyer.

Other issues the prenuptial agreement should address are the division of the martial home, if any, that may have been acquired by either of the parties prior to the relationship. The agreement can outline the division of mortgage payments, the proportionate shares of ownership, special equity interests in the event the property is sold and may also include a complete waiver of any right to the marital property. This can be a very important provision in states that have a homestead provision that restricts or prohibits the devise (gift at death) or transfer of the property during lifetime. Some states have laws that prohibit married couples from negotiating the division of property unless it is in done within the context of a domestic relations court divorce proceeding.

Many people take the position that "the house was mine before we got married, I should be able to do whatever I want to with it." Unfortunately, state law may dictate a different outcome if the parties have not negotiated this prior to marriage. For example, once married, a homestead property cannot be transferred or mortgaged during lifetime without the consent of the spouse and at death there is a prohibition on the transfer of homestead property if the deceased is survived by a spouse or minor child(ren). A complete discussion of these issues is beyond the scope of this book. However, the point is to suggest that you should investigate these issues prior to marriage and not wait until it's too late to do anything about it.

The division of income taxes should also be addressed in a prenuptial agreement. Will you file married filing separately, or jointly? Can the decision be made on a year-to-year basis depending on your financial circumstances? This provision should also spell out if you file jointly how the tax liability will be shared, as well as any refunds that may be paid. It should also address how an IRS audit and resulting liability, penalty and/or interest should be allocated.

You will also want to carefully consider whether you want to waive any rights you may have to inherit from your future spouse. If this is a first marriage and you are willing to waive certain rights to assets in the event of divorce, you may not be so willing to waive those rights in the event of death. Many states have protective statutes, called the "elective share," that prohibit a spouse from disinheriting a spouse with her permission. Essentially, the elective share represents a percentage (often 30%) of the deceased spouse's estate that may also include the marital residence. This is an oversimplification but it is important to understand that you should not waive this right without proper consultation with legal counsel.

You may also be asked to waive your right to serve as personal representative, guardian or healthcare surrogate for your spouse. Usually this issue arises if you are entering into a second or more marriage and there are grown children from the first marriage. A colleague has a client where this turned out to be a very valuable provision. The husband was entering a second marriage late in life at a time when it was already clear that he was declining mentally. The prenuptial agreement provided that his new spouse would waive her right to serve as his personal representative in the event of death and as his guardian in the event of disability. As his mind has continued to fail and her desire to gain control of the family assets has become more evident, this provision is preventing her from controlling assets she might otherwise have had access to.

One right you don't have the ability to waive is the entitlement to child support. Child support is a right that actually belongs to the child and not to the parent. This issue is not properly addressed in a prenuptial agreement as the law, facts and circumstances at the time of divorce will dictate whether either party will have an obligation regarding child support.

Life Alliance Agreements™

Couples in an unmarried relationship who are not contemplating marriage in the near future can't create a prenuptial agreement for a "someday" marriage. The law requires that a prenuptial be made in specific contemplation of marriage—where it is in the near future.

Some committed couples do not intend to marry soon or ever. Others cannot legally marry as in the case of same sex couples, in most states. Therefore, a prenuptial is not an option for them. However, they should consider creating what we call a *Life Alliance Agreement*, an agreement that can contain many of the same clauses and provisions as a prenuptial agreement but is not dependent upon a marital relationship.

The difficulty for an unmarried relationship is that there are few, if any, laws that provide protection for unmarried partners. Therefore, most protections have to be created in the form of agreements between the partners. Any agreements regarding division of assets and waiver of rights should only be done after consultation with financial and legal advisors. The agreements must be executed with certain legal formalities to be enforceable. In addition, there are some states that have taken a dim view of the enforcement of relationship contracts between unmarried couples. Here, greater creativity may be required in order to produce the legal result desired by the couple.

For more information regarding the legal and financial hurdles presented to unmarried couples, read *Loving Without a License: An Estate Planning Survival Guide for Unmarried Couples and Same Sex Partners.* Visit *www.LovingWithoutALicense.com.*

Special Concerns for Business Owners or Family Businesses

Business Owners

If you are a business owner, part of your basic protection package should be a well-drafted Buy-Sell business succession agreement supported by financial strategies such as long-term disability insurance, business interruption insurance and life insurance. You can never predict when your business partner will become disabled, die or simply decide to leave the business. A business succession agreement will set forth the wishes of all the business owners regarding the terms and conditions under which the business will be sold or purchased depending on the occurrence of an unexpected event. Financial strategies and tools are necessary to provide the liquidity and/or funding to accomplish your stated goals.

Business owners, or children of owners of family businesses, have additional challenges if they want to protect the company from the disruption caused by the divorce proceedings of one of its owners, the breakup of life partners or even the divorce of an owner's adult child. Unfortunately, "relationship protection" is sometimes overlooked as a potential threat when financial planners create an 'asset protection" plan for a business owner. A thorough discussion of this topic is beyond the scope of this book. Some of these concepts are listed below to illustrate how some assets can be threatened by a division of assets in the dissolution of a relationship and why a succession agreement is essential for all business owners.

Business owners who reinvest assets in the business and maintain few assets independent of the business can be placing the business in harm's way during the dissolution of a relationship. It is important to take stock of all your assets to make sure they will be protected in the event the relationship fails.

Children of a business founder are often employed in the family business. Sometimes they are considered a key employee which means they hold an important management and ownership position within the company. Key employees who receive stock as part of their compensation package should have a written agreement with their spouses that the stock was not purchased with marital assets and was intended as a gift to the key employee rather than an employment benefit.

The method for valuing a business should be set forth in a business succession agreement. This could mean the agreement sets forth a formula or appraisal or other method by which the value of the business is set.

Limited Liability Companies and Family Limited Partnerships

Limited liability companies and family limited partnerships have become popular legal structures for protecting assets from the potential claims of creditors. The implementation of these structures will vary from state to state based on the strength of state laws and require that you follow precise creation and administration procedures. Entities can offer additional asset protection for individuals and business owners, while offering opportunities for wealth transfer to children or other family members. An in depth discussion of advanced asset protection techniques is beyond the scope of this chapter and this book, but be advised that your legal and financial professionals can provide you with guidance in creating legal structures to accomplish your goals.

The financial and legal strategies discussed in this chapter are protections to safeguard your wealth and your health. They are an essential part of The Confidence Continuum because they can give you the confidence that you can control your assets while you are alive and well; protect yourself and your family in the event of disability; and at death, give what you have, to whom you want, when you want; and do so efficiently and safely, managing both the financial and emotional costs associated with disability and death.

Where to Keep Your Directives

Where you keep your directives could be the difference between making important decisions immediately or only after a delay. It is important to understand that healthcare directives are only useful if they are available to your agents and healthcare providers in a medical emergency. Copies are as good as the originals for healthcare directives. Therefore, you should provide a copy to each agent you have named and to your doctors. You should also have one readily available for yourself, particularly if you travel. Always take your healthcare directives with you if you have scheduled medical procedures.

For a small subscription fee, you can file your financial and healthcare directives with a repository company. This means your instructions can be available via fax to healthcare providers worldwide, 24 hours a day and seven days a week. The repository gives you a wallet card to keep with your insurance card. The wallet card has instructions on how to obtain the forms. See *www.docubank.com* or *www.MyPersonalWishes.com* or your legal advisor for more information on services of this kind.

Updating, Maintenance and Family Education

Many people view estate planning as a single transaction, something you get done and then don't have to worry about any more. This is especially true if the initial planning process was emotionally traumatic—it isn't an experience you want to have to repeat. You may be surprised to learn then that all estate planning requires ongoing updating, maintenance and family education. Creating your plan is simply the first step in a lifetime process.

There are a number of factors that can influence an estate plan over time—the four L's:

1) Changes in your Life— your family or financial circumstances;
2) Changes in the Law—both state and federal laws—that may affect the long-term operation of our plan;
3) Changes in your Lawyer and their scope of experience; and
4) Change in your Legacy—the way you want to leave assets to family or other beneficiaries

Changes in Your Family or Financial Circumstances

The first type of change an estate plan faces is change that directly affects you and your family, both personal and financial. The problems with this type of change arise as a result of your role as expert on yourself and your family. There is no way for your attorney and other planning professionals to learn about these changes unless you tell them. Our experience has been that most people don't communicate regularly with their professional advisors, thereby putting their estate plan in danger of failing. Sometimes, people are discouraged from communicating with their professional advisors because of the actual or perceived cost of communicating changed circumstances. In other words, people tend to communicate with their advisors less when they know there is an invoice attached.

Changes in the Law

The second type of change an estate plan faces is change to either state or federal laws, including the tax laws, changes to program benefits, limitations and restrictions or laws that can affect the personal planning protections provided in your estate plan. Laws today change very rapidly and only advisors that are actively engaged in estate planning may be aware of all of the changes and the impact on your planning circumstances.

Changes in Your Lawyer's Scope of Experience and Strategies

The third type of change an estate plan faces is change in your lawyer or professional advisor's experience. Many professionals are committed to constantly improving their practices, their knowledge and the quality of their planning. Others continue to practice the same way they always have. Does your attorney have years of cumulative experience or are they still doing things the same old way? In Chapter Nine look for guidance on evaluating your lawyer and other trusted advisors commitment to excellence.

Changes in Your Legacy

As you transition through the various phases of your life and make progress on The Confidence Continuum, you may discover that your idea of legacy will mature over time. Your legacy is the what, the who and the how of how you want to pass on your values and your valuables. Because your legacy does change dramatically over time, making sure that your estate plan is a true reflection of your goals becomes increasingly more important.

An Estate Planning Solution

It's not about documents—it's about results! The key to proper estate planning is clear, comprehensive, customized instructions for your own care and that of your loved ones. These instructions can be included in your Will or Trust and in your disability directives. Regardless of the type of planning you've chosen, most people are best served with an estate planning process that revolves around a strategy that implements a commitment to keep your plan updated and maintained and your family well-educated.

We recommend that you revisit your estate planning not less than every two to three years. Take the time to sit down with your lawyer and review the decisions that you made previously to make sure they are still consistent with your goals and your life. If you acquire new assets, make sure that you are reviewing asset ownership and beneficiary designation impacts and how they integrate with your written estate plan.

The National Network of Estate Planning Attorneys informally polled its clients and discovered that, on average, people update their estate plans every 19.6 years! Has anything changed in the last 20 years that may have affected your estate plan? The last 10? The last five? How about in the last year? Estate plans that don't work when expected result in lost benefits for loved ones, can result in litigation and worse, may cause family turmoil that undermines the structure of the family.

Last but not least, you and your family should continuously strive for additional education on matters related to your financial and estate plans. Knowing what to do and how to do it are key components to creating plans that are designed to work for you and your family. Education is especially valuable at times when families are not operating in crises mode—everyone learns better in a stress-free environment. Yet, our experience indicates that most families learn what they need to know at a time when they are least receptive to learning it—at the time of need when there has been a family crisis.

If your planning professional doesn't offer a formal updating, maintenance and education program, discipline yourself to review your plan on a systematic basis. As you prepare to have your annual tax return prepared, this is a good time to get out your estate planning documents and review them with your professional team. Financial advisors generally offer or require annual reviews with their clients, this gives you a good opportunity to review the performance of your financial portfolio and to discuss and measure whether your investment strategy is still consistent with your long-term goals.

So far, you've learned valuable lessons on creating and protecting wealth. The next step on The Confidence Continuum is wealth independence. ✳

chapter five

W e a l t h   I n d e p e n d e n c e

You created it. You protected it. When do you reach independence? What does "wealth independence" mean? Just like our earlier comparison of wealth to beauty, independence is in the eye of the beholder. Does it represent control, as in "autonomy?" Is it defined by dollars? If yes, how many dollars? Are these dollars for buying basics, extras or both? Or does it involve some other standard?

For our purposes, *Wealth Independence* represents the phase where the core financial vehicles have produced sufficient financial heft to offer a woman a measure of flexibility and resilience regarding lifestyle choices and quality. For example, in this phase she is well insured from loss due to natural disaster, business reversal, loss of her spouse from death or divorce or other unexpected catastrophic financial events. She is no longer living pay check to pay check. Her legal and financial planning provided her with the wherewithal to maintain autonomy under most circumstances. Wealth independence appears on The Confidence Continuum after sound wealth creation and wealth protection principles are implemented so that you can feel confident about remaining in control and maintaining your level of achievement.

ACHIEVING YOUR GOALS

One of the reasons you've reached the phase of wealth independence is that you've avoided the top ten estate planning mistakes set forth in *Appendix A*. An independent woman understands the potential mistakes and uses a combination of financial and legal strategies to achieve independence.

Retirement

You've worked hard, you've paid your dues and retirement is in your dreams of your future. What kind of legal and financial issues does that raise? As you can imagine, there are more than a few.

The prospect of retirement is exciting. Finally you'll have all the time to do all the things you've never had the time to do before. We hope this is true. Many of our clients have found that they are busier than ever in retirement and can't seem to put their finger on how they spend their day. Many remark that they don't know how they ever had time to work. That's a great sentiment and one we are both looking forward to.

Financially there are a number of issues that are before you. Depending on your age, you may be eligible for Social Security benefits. Often the dilemma is whether to take your benefits at the earliest age possible or wait until you can get a higher payout. There are a couple of different schools of thought. One is going to depend on whether you intend to work at all—as in some part-time type of employment or if you intend to retire cold turkey. You can consult with a financial advisor who should be able to run the numbers for you to determine which route will be in your best interest. Some people have determined that it is better to start taking their Social Security now rather than wait in the event they don't live until a later date. That's always a possibility but not necessarily the only reason to postpone receipt of your Social Security.

Another factor that will play into your decision making is how much money you have saved during your working years. Do you have a 401(k), 403(b), IRA or other investment assets accumulated over time? Did your employer offer a pension plan? Now the advice we gave when you first left home as a young adult looks like good advice—start young, save as much as you can—preferably on a tax deferred basis—and watch how it grows for you over the years. If you haven't done a good job at saving, you may find that your Social Security is one of your only sources of income. This can be a dangerous position to be in because generally Social Security is not going to be sufficient to meet all of your needs. There are far too many people in this country relying solely on their Social Security.

If you've invested wisely over the years you may find that your Social Security is just a nice supplement to your retirement income and you may have more flexibility in determining when you will begin your payments. People who work while receiving Social Security retirement benefits can trigger taxes on their benefits if their income exceeds specified levels. Be sure to consult with your tax professional to make sure you don't get surprised at the end of the year.

If you've decided not to completely retire but just to change gears, well good for you. You may live a longer, happier and healthier life by staying actively engaged in the business world surrounded by younger people and challenges that will keep you young.

Retirement Savings

The most common forms of retirement savings are going to be your 401(k), 403(b) and/or your Individual Retirement Account (IRA)—either Roth or traditional. You can start making penalty free withdrawals from these accounts upon attaining age 59. Before 59 the penalty is 10% of the amount withdrawn. There are some strategies for taking penalty-free withdrawals prior to attaining age 59. If you need to make early withdrawals, be sure to consult with your financial professional to discuss the strategy that will be best for you.

You **must** start taking withdrawals from your retirement accounts by April 1 of the year following the year you turn 70. The government is bound and determined to start collecting the deferred income tax at some point and this is where the rubber meets the road. At this point you have to take out what's called your Required Minimum Distribution or RMD. It is based on a life expectancy table which is structured so that you take out a certain amount each year and if all projections work out perfectly, you'll take your last distribution in the last year of your life. As you know, projections are just projections and they may not necessarily be true or accurate in your case. You don't want to ignore this IRS rule though because the penalty for not taking your RMD is 50% of the amount not withdrawn! That's a high price to pay, and we don't recommend it.

There are a lot of IRS rules regarding naming beneficiaries for your retirement accounts. A full discussion of these rules is beyond the scope of this book, but be advised that you should seek professional legal and/or financial assistance in making these decisions. Don't forget, however, that your beneficiary designations need to be well-thought out and consistent with the overall intent of your estate plan. Your estate planning attorney and your financial advisor need to be in communication to make sure everyone is on the same page. Generally, however, if you have a Will, you'll name the same beneficiaries for your retirement account that you named in your Will (Note: remember not to name any minor beneficiaries outright.) If you've done a Living Trust, generally your trust will be the primary beneficiary of your retirement plan with named individuals as an alternate choice. Don't let anyone tell you that you can't name a trust as a retirement account beneficiary. You can, but you have to know and follow the rules.

Healthcare

If you are 65 or older when you retire, you will most likely qualify for Medicare, a federal health insurance program. However, if you retire before age 65, you'll need some way to pay for your healthcare until Medicare kicks in. Some employers offer generous health insurance coverage to their retiring employees, but this is the exception rather than the rule. Plus, many employers that provided health coverage to retired employees are seeking ways to modify that commitment. If your employer doesn't extend health benefits to you, you may need to buy a private health insurance policy (which will be costly) or extend your employer-sponsored coverage through COBRA.

Although Medicare is going to be useful for health insurance purposes, it won't pay for long-term care costs, such as may be required if you have to go in a nursing home. We'll spend more time talking about how to pay for long-term care below.

Most Americans automatically become entitled to Medicare when they turn 65. If you're already receiving Social Security benefits, you won't even have to apply—you'll be automatically enrolled in Medicare.

However, you will have to decide whether you need only Part A coverage (which is premium-free for most retirees) or if you will also want Part B coverage, which comes at an additional cost. Part A, commonly referred to as the hospital insurance portion of Medicare, can help pay for your home healthcare, hospice care, and inpatient hospital care. Part B helps cover other medical care costs such as physician care, laboratory tests, and physical therapy. You might also choose to enroll in a managed care plan or private fee-for-service plan under Medicare Part C (Medicare Advantage) if you want to pay fewer out-of-pocket healthcare costs. If you don't already have adequate prescription drug coverage, you should also consider joining a Medicare prescription drug plan offered in your area by a private company or insurer that has been approved by Medicare.

Even with Medicare, all of your healthcare expenses won't be covered. For some types of care, you'll have to satisfy a deductible and make co-payments. That's one reason why you may consider purchasing what's known as a Medigap policy.

There are 12 standard Medigap policies available. Each of these policies offers certain basic core benefits, and all but the most basic policy (Plan A) offer various combinations of additional benefits designed to cover what Medicare does not. Although not all Medigap plans are available in every state, you should be able to find a plan that best meets your needs and your budget.

When you first enroll in Medicare Part B at age 65 or older, you have a six-month Medigap open enrollment period. During that time, you have the right to buy the Medigap policy of your choice from a private insurance company, regardless of any health problems you may have. The company cannot refuse you a policy or charge you more than other open enrollment applicants. If you wait, you may not be able to qualify later.

All Medicare beneficiaries are eligible to join a Medicare prescription drug plan offered by private companies or insurers that have been approved by Medicare. Although these plans vary in price and benefits, they all cover a broad number of brand name and generic drugs available at local pharmacies or through the mail. Medicare prescription drug coverage is voluntary, but if you decide to join a plan, keep in mind that some plans cover more drugs or offer a wider selection of pharmacies (for a higher premium) than others. You can get information and help with comparing plans on the Medicare website, www.medicare.gov, or by calling a Medicare counselor at 1-800-Medicare.

Long-Term Care

If you haven't considered the purchase of long-term care insurance before now, there's no time like the present. The younger and healthier you are when you purchase it, the less expensive it will be. Before we go any further, let's make sure that the whole idea of long-term care is clear. Long-term care is either in-home or other full-time care in an assisted living facility or nursing home because you are no longer capable of performing all of the activities of daily living. Activities of daily living are in and of themselves a defined term and include such things as eating, bathing, dressing, toileting, transferring from a bed or a chair, grooming, and walking. Generally when you can no longer do two or more of the above named activities, you qualify for benefits under most long-term care policies.

This year, according to *www.medicare.gov*, about nine million men and women over the age of 65 will need long-term care. By 2020, 12 million older Americans will need long-term care. Most will be cared for at home and family and friends will be the sole caregivers for 70 percent of the elderly. A study by the U.S. Department of Health and Human Services says that people who reach age 65 will likely have a 40 percent chance of entering a nursing home. About 10 percent of the people who enter a nursing home will stay there five years or more.

There are essentially three ways you can pay for long-term care. First you can save enough money over your lifetime to pay for it yourself. Most people don't feel like they have enough money saved unless they have more than a million dollars. Don't forget that long-term care facilities generally cost about $6,000 per month on average and the cost isn't going down. A one year stay in a long-term care facility and you've wiped out $72,000 of your hard-earned savings.

The second way you can pay for long-term care is to insure against the risk. That means purchasing a long-term care policy that will pay for some or all of your long-term care costs in the event you find yourself unable to care for yourself. Insurance is generally a "pennies on the dollar" approach to paying for something that costs more than you may be able to pay for independently. It works on the same concept as life insurance, car insurance and homeowner's insurance. Statistically a certain number of people will require long-term care for a specific period of time. Insurance companies know how to calculate these risks and the corresponding premiums and then create products to sell to the public. The number of policies on the market today can be mind boggling. Again, it is critically important that you work with a professional well-schooled in long-term care so that you can navigate through the various options that are available and make the best decisions for you. A person in their forties who qualifies for a group policy may find that their monthly premium is less than $50 per month. At that rate, you may be able to afford to pay coverage for a long time and still come out ahead if you need long-term care in the future. Look at your lifestyle and decide whether you expose yourself to a higher than normal level of risk for possible serious injury. And don't forget, that if you are under age 65, you have a greater likelihood of becoming disabled, than simply dying.

The third way you can pay for long-term care is by relying on good 'ole Uncle Sam and hoping you qualify for a governmental benefit program like Medicaid. There's nothing simple about qualifying for Medicaid and you have to essentially impoverish yourself before you can qualify for the program. There are both income and asset requirements. The Medicaid qualification rules are constantly changing and the assistance of an elder law attorney who practices in this area is going to be very important.

We would rather see people insure against the possible risk of long-term care than to rely on the existence of a governmental program. You may not get the type or kind of care that you want under a government program and there is no guarantee that a program that meets your needs is going to be available when you need it. In addition, Medicaid may not provide the same quality of care that you would want if you were paying for it independently. Further, many people confuse the idea of Medicare with Medicaid and they just aren't the same thing. They don't offer the same rules for qualification or the same type of benefits.

Medicare and Long-Term Care

While there are a variety of ways to pay for long-term care, it is important to think ahead about how you will fund the care you get. Generally, Medicare doesn't pay for long-term care, either in-home or in a nursing home. Medicare pays only for a medically necessary skilled nursing facility or home healthcare. However, you must meet certain conditions for Medicare to pay for these types of care. Most long-term care is to assist people with support services such as activities of daily living like dressing, bathing, and using the bathroom. Medicare doesn't pay for this type of care called "custodial care." Custodial care (non-skilled care) is care that helps you with activities of daily living. It may also include care that most people do for themselves, for example, diabetes monitoring. Some of the new Medicare Advantage Plans (formerly Medicare + Choice) may offer limited skilled nursing facility and home care (skilled care) coverage if the care is medically necessary. However, you may still have to pay some of the costs.

Medicaid and Long-Term Care

Medicaid is a state and Federal government program that pays for certain health services and nursing home care for older people with low incomes and limited assets. In most states, Medicaid also pays for some long-term care services at home and in the community. Who is eligible and what services are covered vary from state to state. Most often, eligibility is based on your income and personal resources. It has been our experience that most people don't work their whole lives to look forward to qualifying for Medicaid—essentially a government welfare program designed for indigent people. Instead, we recommend sound financial planning techniques that will help you avoid the need for this type of program.

Housing

After retirement, your housing needs may change. You may be tired of doing yard work or living in a big house. You might want to retire to sunny

Florida or a climate like Arizona. You might even choose to live close to your children or grandchildren. Or, your circumstances may dictate that you will live in an assisted living facility or nursing home. Many older retirees elect to remain in their own home for as long as possible. We know of seniors in their late nineties who are still quite capable of living at home on their own.

If you want to stay in your home you'll have to consider whether you are capable of taking care of yourself. If you can't, perhaps a family member or relative could help you with your household chores, laundry and shopping. Can you afford to hire someone who can do some of the chores you are no longer capable of doing? Is there a source of reliable transportation nearby if you are unable to drive? Do you have physical needs that will require a renovation or modification of your home?

If you can't stay at home, can you live with one or more of your children? Some of our clients have enough children that they are able to rotate from child to child on a frequent enough basis that no one ever gets tired of having a visitor. If you need to live with your child full-time, there will be a number of issues to consider. Will you have the privacy you need and deserve? Will you be the on-hand babysitter and/or cleaning lady, and is this a responsibility you are willing to take on?

What are the emotional consequences of living with your child? Is this an adjustment that both you and your child are willing to make? What type of relationship do you enjoy with your child? Some parents promise to never live with any of their children—it's not how they envision their retirement years. Some studies have indicated it may be healthier to live with people your own age so that you maintain a network of friends and have opportunities to participate in regular activities outside the home.

You'll also want to talk about important financial issues with your child before you agree to move in. This conversation will help avoid conflicts or hurt feelings later. Things you want to discuss will include how much you will be expected to contribute toward household expenses. If you will not be expected to contribute, how will that make you feel? Is your child financially capable of taking on another person in their household? Do you and your child have similar philosophies regarding spending or are you likely to be critical of each other's habits? The answers to these questions will help determine whether living with your child is even a viable solution. Some families feel that their parents have no other choice because they haven't saved sufficiently to afford an alternative lifestyle.

If you decide that living on your own and living with your child are not available options, perhaps you have a close friend who is in a similar situation and the two of you can help each other out. If you have enough friends, you may be able to enjoy an interesting lifestyle living in different parts of the country as you move from your home to her home, etc. Or, you may consider an assisted living facility.

We've visited some assisted living facilities that were so nice we were ready to move in right away! Most provide some sort of apartment type room, housekeeping, some or all meals, social interaction and transportation. A primary focus of assisted living tends to be social activities rather than medical support so you should be able to care for yourself. Assisted living options can either cater to a large number of people or be smaller more intimate type settings. Many allow small pets such as cats or dogs—an important element that can contribute to a healthier, longer life.

Financial arrangements at assisted living facilities can vary greatly from a monthly rental-type arrangement to a buy-in type of down payment and then regular monthly payments. Be sure to read the contract carefully and don't hesitate to ask an attorney to read it for you if you are unsure of what you are signing. It is always better to ask for advice before you sign something than after—cheaper too!

As we've already mentioned, Medicare and Medicaid usually don't pay for care in an assisted living facility so in all likelihood you'll be paying for the cost out of your own pocket. Sometimes children are willing and able to provide financial assistance to make sure that you are well taken care of.

If living alone, living with your children or a friend and living in an assisted living facility aren't options, then a nursing home would generally be the housing choice of last resort. We've met few people in our lives that say they want to live in a nursing home. However, the reality is that as we grow older a nursing home may be in some of our futures.

Nursing homes

Nursing homes are usually licensed residential facilities that offer 24-hour supervised care and access to medical care. There are typically three levels of care that are provided: skilled nursing care, intermediate care, and custodial care. Most people that live in a nursing home do so because they are unable to live alone or in an assisted living facility; instead they need more care than can be provided in either of those two settings.

In a nursing home you might find that instead of having your own private room that you are sharing a room with another person. This is one way the nursing homes try and keep the costs down. This is an important privacy issue to consider when considering how you might pay for nursing home care. Can you afford to live in a private room or will your finances dictate that you share a room with another person?

Choosing a nursing home can be a difficult decision. Often, nursing homes are chosen out of necessity rather than as part of a planned decision-making process. Don't forget the adage, "Be nice to your children, they'll be selecting your nursing home." Sadly, there is some truth to this statement as many children find themselves in a position to either select or assist in the selection of a nursing home for their parent(s). We suggest that you try and plan ahead for this possibility when you are still really well. Visit the nursing homes in your area to see whether they offer the services and quality of care that you will be comfortable with. Does it feel like a hospital or does it feel like home? Will the facility permit your family to show up without advance notice so they can spot check the type of services you are being provided? Nursing home litigation has become popular over the past several years and more nursing homes than ever are losing their ability to purchase insurance. Many are now self-insured, a situation that might not be in your best interest if the facility is not well-run.

Although none of us wants to believe that we will ever live in a nursing home, the facts just don't support this theory. Remember Estate Planning Mistake #10 listed in Appendix A. If and when retirement or healthcare or a change of residence becomes an issue, you should make sure you review your directives with your financial and legal team. Planning must be an ongoing process to make sure you can maintain your wealth independence.

Chapter Eight regarding life crisis outlines more information regarding disability programs such as Social Security Disability Income (SSDI) and Supplemental Security Income (SSI).

Congratulations! Wealth independence represents the phase where you've reached the point that the accumulation and protection of wealth doesn't take all your time and all your resources—you've become independent in the sense that your primary financial goals have been achieved and you are reaping the benefits. You are now in a position to consider the final phase of The Confidence Continuum—*Wealth Legacy.* ✖.

chapter six

W e a l t h   L e g a c y

Wealth Legacy represents the phase where a woman is in a position to create a lasting legacy that leaves not only her valuables, but also her values, for others and the causes she supports. Her financial and legal strategies are designed to help her lead by example and contribute to others through her experience and lessons she can share. Winston Churchill said, "We make our living by what we get. We make a life by what we give."

But say the word "legacy" and most people think of money that is inherited. In their mind's eye the sum is usually large and it is something that happens to someone else. Legacy is a term most people don't associate with themselves either in the giving or receiving. It is defined by Merriam—Webster's Online dictionary as *1*. A gift by Will especially of money or other personal property: Bequest. *2*. Something transmitted by or received from an ancestor or predecessor or from the past.

For our purposes, legacy is more than just our valuables or the tangible things we leave behind when we die. It includes our values as well which can help future generations to build a good, strong future where they contribute to loved ones and others, continuing to "pay it forward."

In fact, a study commissioned by Allianz Life Insurance Company of North America with Age Wave revealed that elders and their boomer children agree that passing on ethics, faith, morals, and religion is *ten* times more important than the financial assets. Yet, the study shows that parents and their children don't discuss those matters in a meaningful way, leading to what the study calls a "Legacy Gap"—a communication gap.

The study says that a meaningful discussion about legacy must include four pillars:

- Values and life lessons
- Fulfilling final wishes and instructions

- Personal possessions of emotional value
- Financial assets

Our values can be expressed in many ways, intentionally and unintentionally. The nature and manner in which assets are bequeathed, given either outright or in trust to others, whether we engaged in careful planning and attention to detail to protect our survivors or cause them to involve the courts, and whether we made charitable gifts to benefit others are just some of the ways we demonstrate our standards and values. We lead by example when we create an estate plan or fail to do so. Our survivors have memories of us after we are gone. We can create good memories that serve as examples to our survivors for generations. Or, we can fail to plan adequately and cause our survivors to look back to their time with us on this earth through a veil of painful memories about how difficult life was when and after we passed away. This is particularly true when the deceased had a long illness leading to death and many assets are consumed by the long-term care needs prior to death. The survivor(s) can be emotionally and physically exhausted and fearful about what their future may hold in terms of being able to support themselves.

By this definition, we all leave a legacy of some kind when we die. It is a bit ironic, however, that most resources covering estate and financial planning or advisors in these fields don't address this aspect of legacy planning except in a cursory or patchy way, if at all, except when it involves high net worth clients. There has been a growing trend in some advisor circles to lead high net worth clients through a "family retreat" to help them articulate what their wealth means to them and what they want it to mean for their survivors. Clearly, advisors to such clients can justify providing this type of extra service as a way to distinguish themselves from product-sales oriented advisors and because the advisor's overall compensation can accommodate this activity.

Advisors to middle and low net worth clients, on the other hand, probably don't feel they can justify the extra effort and resources required to lead clients through this kind of introspective discussion. It might not occur to them that their clients would be interested in this type of service. After all, it can be challenging enough to get clients motivated to complete their essential legal directives! Plus, many advisors are not likely to offer "services" that don't directly support the tangible products they provide such as a legal directives or insurance products. Unfortunately, that kind of "all or nothing" thinking can lead them to overlook ways to deepen the legacy planning experience for the person making the plan and for the beneficiaries of the plan. Thoughtful and resourceful advisors can and do help families consider more than "who gets my stuff" without the time and dollar investment of a family retreat. The resources listed in Chapter Ten include some advisor groups that train advisors to help families overcome the Legacy Gap described in the Allianz study. (See also www.SunbrigeStrategies.com).

Outside of the training such programs provide advisors, there are no one-stop-shopping guides that outline the many ways to plan for the full range of a legacy, which we will call a Full Dimension Legacy, from the valuables to the values. This chapter will outline some of the things you can consider and discuss with your advisors. You should also review the *Top 10 Estate Planning Mistakes* in Appendix A. It is also helpful to apply the "golden rule" and think about how you, if you were the survivor, would want to experience a loved one's passing—everything from knowing who to call, to the financial logistics, to the details about your obituary. But first, it helps to have a framework within which to organize the types of matters you should consider. You don't have to plan on all levels. Rather, you can pick and choose the kind of details that appeal to you *a la carte*. At least you will have been in a position to include or exclude these details in your plan instead of having them excluded because no one made you aware that they were possible options.

The Full Dimension Legacy™ Framework

Planning a Full Dimension Legacy™ beyond mere "stuff" requires you to consider the four pillars described in the Allianz study. We think of the three dimensions of any legacy: inspirational, practical and tangible.

Inspirational involves personal letters intended for heirs and future generations when you are gone. This might include children, grandchildren or nieces and nephews. It might include family members who are too young to talk or who are yet to be born. These letters can express your personal philosophy and wisdom about life, stories, things you would express if you were on earth to do so.

Practical involves the logistics of memorial instructions, funerals, obituaries, lists that detail your assets and the location of important papers.

Tangible involves our "stuff," from the money we give at death to the personal belongings of sentimental value. It involves not only the specific items but the manner in which those items are given, such as outright distribution to heirs or for their benefit in trust.

This chapter only provides the general parameters at each level. The detail and depth of the planning is up to individual taste and imagination. The more detailed, the more survivors will have a strong "compass point" to guide them. Some resources for additional guidance are included in Chapter Ten. (See *www.careofdying.org*).

Inspirational

Family Lore and History

In today's mobile society many families are geographically spread out unlike their parents' and grandparents' generations. They don't have the day-to-day interaction that living nearby permits, including the luxury of time to share seemingly insignificant moments, but moments that can provide memories rich with personal detail and nostalgia. Unfortunately, this can mean that much of the family lore, stories and history behind family heirlooms and silly "stuff" isn't communicated. When elders pass away, so does much of their knowledge of family history and the history behind physical items such as jewelry and photographs passed to the next generation. How many families have old photos of ancestors but no clear recollection about who is in the photo?

Many women are postponing marriage and/or their child rearing years until their careers are established. This can mean that the time grandparents have with grandchildren is limited to the children's pre-adult years—before the grandchildren can appreciate that they need to remember the stories and histories the grandparents share. This communication gap isn't confined to grandparents and grandchildren, however. Adult children can miss out on the family history behind a ring or a table or other tangible item that is passed to them at death. Programs like *The Antique Roadshow* prove that the stories behind "things" can be as interesting, or more so, than the items themselves and can sometimes add monetary value to the item as well.

We can overcome legacy communication gaps by creating letters to children, grandchildren and others. These are sometimes called "ethical wills" although they are not wills in any sense of the technical term. There are some resources listed in Chapter Ten that can give you some guidance for these letters.

Practical

Location Lists

One of the heartaches many probate and estate settlement advisors see families experience, on top of grieving the loss of a loved one, involves what is sometimes called the "morbid scavenger hunt." This occurs when surviving family members try to remember which accounts the deceased owned and where the paperwork is filed. Creating a detailed asset list and accompanying location list is a thoughtful gesture and can spare survivors anxiety about overlooking something important. Remember the paper trail described in the Top Ten Estate Planning Mistakes in Appendix A and create a clear trail for survivors.

Memorial Instructions

Part of thoughtful estate planning includes preparing your funeral and memorial arrangements rather than leaving this task to survivors who must make important personal and financial decisions while trying to cope emotionally with the grieving process. It can be another example of leading by example; demonstrating care through attention to detail so to spare survivors from having to make these decisions during a difficult time. This can be particularly helpful to family members who are far flung and have limited time to make arrangements and pay respects.

The arrangements can include everything from cremation or burial to the music played at a religious service to the outfit you want to be dressed in for a wake. Although state law sets forth who can make these decisions if you fail to do so, it makes sense to provide something in writing that outlines your wishes. It saves your survivors from trying to guess what your wishes would be if you haven't communicated these details to them. In an unmarried relationship, state laws will not allow unmarried partners as authorized decision-makers. Things can be further complicated, if your blood relatives have reservations about your relationship. In this case, state law could authorize family members to dictate your funeral arrangements over the objections of your partner.

This writing of your memorial instructions is called a precatory letter. It is not legally binding but is normally honored *if* your survivors know about it in time. This letter should set forth what you want done with your remains: burial, cremation, plastination a la Body Worlds (the international exhibition of whole bodies preserved in a special plastic process for educational display and instruction), or other form of disposition. If you want your ashes scattered someplace, you will need to check with your state laws to confirm where cremains can legally be scattered.

Paying for your final arrangements is another thoughtful gesture. It will save survivors from having to make these difficult decisions during the grieving process and will reduce the likelihood that they will be subject to sales pressures to be extravagant out of guilt. Prepaid arrangements might not be "portable" to other locations if you move to another state so make sure you factor this into your decision-making process.

It seems more and more common for people to specify charitable memorial gifts in lieu of flowers. Decide if this is something you want to mention and include it in your memorial instructions letter.

Obituary

We all have read obituaries that are perfunctory and some that are inspirational. Many newspapers are open to printing prepared obituaries. Choose a picture you like and write the essential information you would like to have included. Writing your obituary doesn't have to be a morbid exercise. In fact, many personal development programs ask participants to do just that to help them focus on what is important in life and what you want to be remembered for. The point is that you can convey by tone and content to family and others what your life "was all about." No one could possibly do it as well as you.

Tangible

The inspirational dimension includes family history or the sentimental significance regarding the giving of tangible assets. However, the type of gift and the manner of distribution of tangible assets can communicate a lot about your values, as well as your priorities.

The following addresses some of the legal-financial-technical aspects of conveying our property and assets to others. It isn't just about the numbers, however. It also requires an understanding about the various legal tools to leverage the most from legal strategies to best aid your loved ones—during life and when you are gone.

Personal Property Memorandum

One aspect of the tangible gifts we might leave is our personal property—affectionately, the "stuff" we buy bigger houses for—our jewelry, furniture, collectibles and heirlooms. The purpose of the Personal Property Memorandum is to specify who is to receive what item of personal property. The intent is to avoid family disagreements or misunderstandings. It is not unusual for multiple family members to make claim to the same sentimental item, all claiming that "Mom said I could have it." Your Personal Property Memorandum is a personal writing that is generally incorporated into your legal directives by statutory reference. One of the benefits is that it can be easily amended if you change your mind or dispose of the item during your lifetime. Many advisors recommend giving away personal property during your lifetime so that you can appreciate the enjoyment the recipient gets from your gift.

You can take the concept of a Personal Property Memorandum a step further and document the history of your collectibles or family heirlooms. It's always a sad day when the story of a precious item is lost because it was never committed to writing or passed down as part of the family history.

In addition to personal property, you will also have your financial assets for distribution, either as gifts during lifetime or after death. How you make these gifts can be unique to you and the legacy you want to leave.

LIFETIME GIFTS

Lifetime giving is one of the best ways to express your gratitude to the world and to make an impact that you can personally experience. You could elect to make gifts to individuals or to charitable organizations. There may be tax advantages, in addition to the personal satisfaction that you gain.

Under current law, an individual can gift up to $12,000 per year to as many people as she likes without incurring any gift tax consequences. These are called "annual exclusion" gifts because they are excluded from any Internal Revenue Service (IRS) reporting requirement or gift tax. In addition, these gifts have no effect on your ability to leave assets at the time of your death. The benefit in making annual exclusion gifts is you get to see the joy in the people you are making the gifts to. You can observe and guide the recipients about the use of the gifts as a way to convey your values. If you plan on making additional gifts to them at your death, it may also be a good way to determine whether they will be good stewards of the money they will receive when you are gone.

Lifetime annual exclusion gifts do not reduce your ability to leave assets at the time of your death. Married couples can give unlimited gifts to each other during life and at death. An individual can leave $2,000,000 to non-spouses at death, free from federal estate tax. This means that you can die owning assets of $2,000,000 or less and your estate (and heirs) will incur no estate tax liability. If your estate exceeds $2,000,000 your heirs will pay an estate tax that starts at 46%—under federal law. States have their own laws regarding estate taxes. Some states have no estate tax and some do. The laws at the federal and state levels are constantly changing, so you'll need to check with your tax or legal professional to make sure you fully understand the current exclusion and exemption amounts.

If you make lifetime gifts that exceed your $12,000 annual exclusion amount, you won't have to pay any tax until you've given away more than $1,000,000. But, you will have an obligation to report the gift to the IRS so they can deduct it from your $2,000,000 exemption at the end of your life. For example, you can give your three children each a gift of $12,000 and you don't have any obligation to tell the IRS about the gift. If you elect to make $20,000 gifts to your children, then you'll have to tell the IRS that you exceeded your annual gift exclusion by $24,000. That's the amount over the annual exclusion gift—$8,000 per child—multiplied by the number of gifts—3—for a total of $24,000. Correspondingly, your $2,000,000 lifetime exemption is now only $1,976,000.

There are exceptions to the annual exclusion gift rules. You can make unlimited gifts for the benefit of health or education as long as those gifts are made directly to the healthcare provider or educational institution. Be careful here, because not all items are covered, like room and board and books. But, if you want to pay your grandchild's college tuition in the amount of $35,000, you'll be able to do so without using any of your $12,000 annual exclusion or $2,000,000 estate tax exemption, provided you make the gift directly to the institution.

If you are not inclined to make gifts to individuals that are outright gifts without strings attached, you could consider making gifts using an irrevocable gifting trust. This type of trust allows you to use your annual exclusion gifts but maintain some measure of control and provide for professional money management. Gifting trusts are a useful tool for making regular periodic gifts to children and grandchildren. Again, there are specific rules you'll need to follow in order to qualify the gifts as annual exclusion gifts, be sure and check with your professional advisors.

Gifts at Death

You might want to make annual gifts to your children or grandchildren but find that you are unwilling or unable to do so because of concerns for the stability of your financial future. Instead, your gifts will have to wait until the end of your lifetime, when all of your needs have been met.

The way you leave assets to your heirs and others is up to you. Many people elect to make outright distributions to their children or grandchildren claiming they "don't want to exert control from the grave." This intent may be noble but also may not be consistent with what might be best for your heirs. In addition to outright distributions, there are an unlimited number of variations on a theme for how you might distribute your assets.

We would like to introduce you to a concept known as the Trust Protection Spectrum™. The Trust Protection Spectrum illustrates the advantages of holding assets in trust for the benefit of a beneficiary either for a period of time or indefinitely during the beneficiary's lifetime.

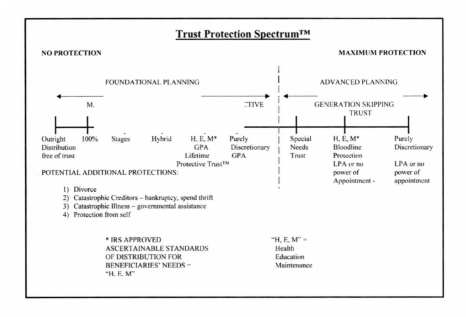

At the far left of the spectrum are outright distribution gifts. This means that once you've passed away, and the administration of your estate is complete, that any gift you are leaving to a beneficiary will be given to them outright. Outright gifts carry with them no form of protection—protection from the beneficiary or protection from the world.

Some beneficiaries will need protection from themselves, either because they have poor money management skills, have drug, alcohol or other dependency disorders or they are developmentally disabled and have special needs. These people need protection from both themselves and from the world. They should not be given outright distributions of assets and should not be permitted to manage the money that you intend to leave for their benefit.

Other beneficiaries don't need personal protection from themselves but could benefit from protection from the world. Protection from the world includes divorce protection, catastrophic creditor protection and catastrophic illness protection. We already know that more than fifty percent (50%) of marriages end in divorce. If an inlaw subsequently becomes an "outlaw" we may not want the inheritance we left to our beneficiary to walk out the door. And there is no specific age when anyone of us becomes immune from divorce, so divorce protection remains important throughout a beneficiary's life.

A catastrophic creditor claim could arise in the event of a financial or business reversal, negligent accident resulting in significant liability exposure, professional malpractice or other unexpected life event resulting in a financial liability. Car accidents are one of the greatest risks we all face. What if your child were driving down the road talking on their cell phone when they were momentarily distracted and killed someone walking on the roadway? Do you think their automobile insurance or homeowner's umbrella insurance policy will be sufficient to cover the potential claim for damages that exists? In all likelihood, the answer is a resounding, "No." If this happens after you've just left your child a significant inheritance, chances are they may lose these assets to satisfy the judgment creditor. Professional liability claims are also on the rise and expose personal assets to attachment by creditors.

If your beneficiary suffers a catastrophic illness, you may want to provide assets for their benefit in trust so that they can benefit from professional money management and administration, while maintaining important public benefits. The existence of a trust will also allow your beneficiary to rely on a successor trustee if they find they are unable to continue to manage their assets as their health deteriorates.

One of the most common trust types used today is the Lifetime Protective Trust™. A Lifetime Protective Trust provides lifetime benefits for your beneficiary—either in the form of personal protection from self or from the world, or both. Generally trust distributions are limited to a broad standard; health, education and maintenance—essentially anything your beneficiary would need to live their life. By keeping assets in trust, rather than distributing them outright, the beneficiary gains the trust protections from the world. If someone other than the beneficiary is the trustee, then you've also added personal protection from the beneficiary, and their corresponding immaturity or other special needs.

You can add flexibility to your trust instructions by being specific with regard to your particular goals and values related to that beneficiary. Trust instructions or additional supplemental instructions can outline your hopes, dreams and aspirations for your beneficiary. We know of one father who limited his son's access to his trust based on the amount of money the son could earn—earn $25,000, get $25,000 in trust distributions. Another grandmother included a stipulation that said, "No trust distributions to beneficiaries with tattoos." While this may sound harsh to some, it was her money and she had a right to condition its use based on her value system.

There may also be tax advantages, such as minimizing exposure to generation skipping taxes that can be achieved through the use of trust planning and adherence to the Trust Protection Spectrum. If part of your legacy includes leaving money not for just one, but many, subsequent generations, a dynasty type trust arrangement may be best for you.

The protections you can provide for your beneficiaries through the use of the Trust Protection Spectrum are benefits they are unable to easily provide for themselves. You can create legal structures for their protection—either from self or from the world—as you determine is in your beneficiary's best interest.

Gifts can also be made to charity at the time of death. These are referred to as testamentary gifts. Many of the charitable trust techniques discussed in this chapter can be created either as lifetime or testamentary trusts. The choice is up to you, the donor, depending on your legacy and other financial factors including lifetime income and taxation goals.

Charitable Gifts

Some people prefer to make charitable giving part of their lifetime philanthropy. In general, people give money and property to charity for a number of reasons. The most common reasons given are:

- The desire to help society by funding a worthy cause
- To enjoy the income and estate tax benefits derived from charitable giving

As a charitable patron, you can make lifetime gifts of cash or property to the charity or charities of your choice. Outright gifts directly to charity or gifts to a charitable remainder trust can help reduce the donor's (the person making the gift) taxable estate not only by the value of the gift but also by the value of the potential growth of the assets over time (appreciation). The Internal Revenue Service, of course, has rules and regulations regarding the total value of lifetime giving you can make and the impact that these gifts will have on your taxable income.

Charitable Trusts

There are a number of types of charitable trusts. The most common are Charitable Remainder Trusts, of which there are several varieties, as well as Charitable Lead Trusts. Essentially, a charitable trust is an irrevocable trust created by a donor during lifetime or by testamentary bequest (at death) for the purpose of providing a stream of income to a named beneficiary for a period of time and, thereafter, the balance of the trusts assets are distributed to a named beneficiary. The identification of the beneficiaries for either the income stream or the remainder is going to depend on the type of charitable trust created, either Charitable Remainder Trust or Charitable Lead Trust. In a Charitable Remainder Trust, the income beneficiary is typically the donor, her spouse or other family members and the remainder beneficiary is a qualifying 501(c)(3) charity. In a Charitable Lead Trust, the income beneficiary is typically the qualifying charity and the remainder beneficiary is the spouse or family members of the donor.

Charitable trusts provide both income tax and estate incentives for the donor. The donor is permitted to take a current income tax deduction for the charitable gift as well as an estate tax deduction at the time of death. The value of the income and estate tax deductions are determined based on the size of the gift, the present value of the stream of income and/or the present value of the remainder interest gift.

Charitable Remainder Trusts

A Charitable Remainder Trust (sometimes referred to as a CRT) is designed to benefit two different parties. The two parties are the individuals receiving the income from the trust and the qualifying charity or charities selected by the donor to receive the balance of the trust assets.

A CRT is a special type of irrevocable trust that pays income to the donor and/or to the donor's family members for their lifetimes or for a specified term of years. After the trust period ends, the assets remaining in the trust are distributed by the trustee to the selected qualified charity or charities. The donor has flexibility in determining what the income distributions will be, who will receive the income from the trust, and what charity or charities will receive the assets when the trust ends.

A CRT can achieve several significant financial and tax goals, including:

- Avoiding capital gains taxes on the value of appreciated assets contributed to the trust.
- An increased stream of income over the lifetime of the donor or other family members.
- An income tax deduction to the donor during life.

There are a number of types of CRTs. The most common are Charitable Remainder Annuity Trusts and Charitable Remainder Unitrusts.

Charitable Remainder Annuity Trust

A Charitable Remainder Annuity Trust (sometimes referred to as a CRAT) is an irrevocable trust that pays a fixed dollar amount each year to a named beneficiary, such as the donor of the trust assets, her spouse, children or others. For example, if $100,000 is donated to a 6% CRAT, the annual income stream would be $6,000. After the death of the income beneficiaries or at the end of a predetermined number of years, the remaining trust assets are distributed to the charity or charities named in the trust.

Once the CRAT is created and the income stream determined, no new additional contributions are allowed. A new charitable trust must be established for additional contributions.

The charitable income tax deduction the donor receives is based on the current value of the charity's right to receive the trust assets at some time in the future.

A number of factors determine this value:

- The estimated length of time the charity has to wait for their remainder distribution. This length of time would be the term of years established by the donor, the donor's lifetime or another person's lifetime.
- The percentage rate payable to the income beneficiaries each year and how frequently the income is paid (annually, quarterly, monthly, etc.)
- The current rate of return on investments as determined by the applicable federal (midterm) rates (AFR). This rate changes on a monthly basis.

If the income from the CRAT is paid to someone other than the donor or the donor's spouse, it may be subject to gift taxation, as discussed above. If certain requirements are met, however, the income gift can qualify for the $12,000 annual gift tax exclusion. There is no limit to the annual dollar amount U.S. spouses can give to each other.

For federal estate tax purposes, the value of the remainder interest passing to the charity is deductible from the donor's gross taxable estate. Your gross taxable estate includes everything you own, everything you control and everything your name is on. That means that the value of your life insurance death benefit, retirement plan accounts including IRAs and 401(k)s in addition to all of your other assets are included for estate tax purposes.

Charitable Remainder Unitrust

A Charitable Remainder Unitrust (sometimes referred to as a CRUT) is an irrevocable trust that pays a fixed percentage of the value of its holdings each year to a named beneficiary such as the donor, her spouse, children or others. For example, if $100,000 is donated to a 6% Charitable Remainder Annuity Trust, the annual income stream the first year would be $6,000. In the second year, if the value of the trust assets grew to $110,000, the annual income stream would be $6,600. Likewise, if in the third year the value of the trust assets decline to $90,000, the annual income stream would be $5,400. Clearly, the income stream can fluctuate with the fluctuating value of the trust assets. After the death of the income beneficiaries or at the end of a predetermined number of years (no more than 20), the remaining trust assets are distributed to the qualifying charity or charities named in the trust.

The trust assets are valued on an annual basis to determine the annual stream of income. Therefore, if the donor desires to add additional contributions in future years, this may be done if desired. There is no necessity to create a new CRUT.

The donor's charitable income tax deduction is determined utilizing the same analysis as for the CRATs. Likewise, the gift tax and estate tax consequences and benefits are the same as for the CRAT.

The benefits of creating a CRT include the following:

- The donor can contribute a highly appreciated, low income producing assets to a CRT and receive a current income tax deduction. This could be especially beneficial to individuals who have accumulated large amounts of corporate stock at a low basis that pays only nominal income.

- The CRT can sell the highly appreciated asset without paying any capital gains tax and can then reinvest the entire proceeds at a higher rate of return.
- The CRT will usually pay the designated income beneficiaries a higher rate of return than the donor previously received on the asset. This, coupled with the income tax deduction, and the avoidance of the capital gains tax on the sale of the appreciated asset can create a substantial increase in cash flow for the donor.

If you are concerned about the value that passes to your family members at death, a Wealth Replacement Trust (an irrevocable trust funded with life insurance) can be used to replace the value of the asset contributed to the Charitable Remainder Trust. This may be a good way to benefit family and charitable purposes at the same time.

Charitable Lead Trusts

Property may be transferred to family members at low gift and estate tax rates by permitting income to be distributed to a qualifying charity over a period of years, and then later pass the balance of the trust assets to family members. This type of irrevocable trust is called a Charitable Lead Trust (sometimes referred to as a CLT). The CLT is the opposite of a CRT because the trustee pays the income first to the charity and the remainder is distributed at the termination of the trust to family members. Properly drafted, CLTs can also result in a current income tax deduction to the donor.

CLTs come in two popular varieties: the Charitable Lead Annuity Trust (sometimes referred to as a CLAT) and the Charitable Lead Unit Trust (sometimes referred to as a CLUT). The CLAT and CLUT operate on the same income distribution principles as the CRATs and CRUTs discussed above. The primary difference between CRTs and CLTs is the timing of the receipt of the charity's interest—today as an income stream or in the future as a remainder interest.

Private Foundations

Although there are many benefits to charitable giving, one concern a donor may express is the loss of control over the money and/or property that is gifted to the charity. To overcome this concern, a donor can create a private foundation that will distribute its donations and income to charitable causes favored by the donor or the donor's family.

A private foundation (sometimes called a Family Foundation) is a charitable organization created and funded by a donor (during life or at death) which is designed to achieve one or more specific charitable purposes. The overall management of the foundation is provided by a board of directors or trustees often selected by the donor and frequently made up of the donor's family members. One reason to choose family members is that the directors or trustees can be paid reasonable compensation for their services.

An individual or a family may establish a foundation to hold the family's charitable gifts. The donor can have complete discretion in distributing the funds to publicly supported qualifying organizations of his or her choice. Contributions to the foundation qualify for income, estate and gift tax charitable deductions, subject to certain restrictions. Families who choose a foundation as part of their estate plan retain maximum control over the distribution of their charitable gift assets, and can use the foundation to teach good stewardship to succeeding generations.

To qualify as a foundation, the federal tax law has specific legal and operating requirements. A private foundation requires the guidance of many trusted advisors including legal, financial and tax professionals. Not all families will have the temperament, the risk tolerance or the ability to effectively administer a family foundation. A family foundation, however, can be a valuable component of a family legacy plan which contemplates the elimination of the estate tax.

Supporting Organizations

An alternative to the private foundation is a supporting organization. The supporting organization has many of the advantages of a private foundation without many of the restrictions. The supporting organization is set up as a trust or nonprofit corporation. The donor retains influence over how charitable funds are used while enjoying the tax benefits allowed for donations to qualifying public charities.

A supporting organization, like a private foundation, is often established and funded by a single individual or family. Unlike foundations, however, supporting organizations are afforded many of the benefits of being a public charity while avoiding the taxes and regulations imposed on foundations.

A supporting organization is typically created as an irrevocable charitable trust. Occasionally, the donor will set up the organization as a nonprofit corporation under state law. At least one public charity (university, hospital, museum, etc.) must be identified in the organizing document as a recipient of the new organization's support. Frequently, the creator and his or her family serve as trustees or directors of the supporting organization, along with the representatives of the charities named.

There are three important tests to quality as a Supporting Organization:

1) The supporting organization must operate exclusively for the benefit of one or more specified public charities.
2) The supporting organization must be operated, supervised, or controlled by, or in connection with, one or more public charities.
3) The supporting organization must not be controlled (directly or indirectly) by a "disqualified person" as defined in IRC Section 4946.

Generally, a supporting organization is accorded the benefits of being a public charity, including:

- Income Tax Deduction for Gifts—a supporting organization is treated the same as for contributions to public charities.
- Not Subject to Private Foundation Excise Taxes—specifically, the prohibitions against self-dealing, minimum distribution requirements, taxes on net investment income, excess business holdings, jeopardizing investments and prohibited expenditures that apply to private foundations do not apply to supporting organizations.

While many people focus on the tax benefits of charitable giving, others are primarily concerned with the loss of control over money and property gifted to a charity. For these persons, the private foundation is usually the preferred choice for achieving their philanthropic goals. The greater control found in a private foundation comes at a cost in the form of greater tax restrictions, significant administrative responsibilities, and increased regulation.

While the creator of a supporting organization does not have the same level of control as the donor who establishes a private foundation, she can still have a significant voice in and an impact on the organization. An unspoken benefit of creating a supporting organization is the opportunity for a donor to involve her children and/or grandchildren in directing the family's philanthropic legacy to public charities in the community. By involving a younger generation in the organization, a donor is sometimes able to convey deeply held family values, while at the same time transferring funds to charitable causes.

Donor Advised Funds

Donor advised funds, although not new in the charitable planning world, have recently been hailed as a vehicle for the modern and moderate philanthropist.

Donors contribute to a managed fund from which grants are made to public charities. The donors have the right to provide advice and recommendations with regard to grant recipients and also to the amount and timing of the grant. The donor is entitled to an immediate charitable contribution deduction upon making the contribution. The trustees of the fund are not obligated to follow the donor's advice and recommendations, although as a practical matter it is expected they will.

Donor advised funds can look very much like private foundations, though on a smaller scale and without the setup and administration costs. Like a private foundation, they conduct no charitable operations themselves, but instead fund other operating charities. They also provide the donor with an element of control similar, but not identical to, that available via a private foundation.

Pooled Income Fund (PIF)

A Pooled Income Fund (PIF) is similar to a Charitable Remainder Trust except that more than one donor is able to make contributions. A public charity establishes and maintains a common investment fund into which donors can transfer assets while retaining a share of the annual income in proportion to the donor's contributions.

The donor's federal income tax deduction is based on the ages of the beneficiary and the highest rate of return paid by the fund over the last three (3) years. The frequency of payments does not affect the income tax deduction.

If the donor causes the income to be paid to someone other than herself, there is the potential for a taxable gift unless certain requirements are met and the income gift can qualify for the $12,000 annual gift tax exclusion.

The value of the asset passing to the PIF is removed from the donor's gross estate for federal estate taxation purposes. The income stream received by the donor, however, could increase her estate unless otherwise consumed. After the life income beneficiary dies, the remaining assets pass to the charitable organization.

Charitable Gift Annuity

A Charitable Gift Annuity (CGA) makes it possible to transfer cash or marketable securities, such as stocks or bonds (including mutual funds) to a charity in exchange for fixed payments that you or someone else you designate will receive for life.

The amount of the annual income received is determined based on the age of the income beneficiary. You get a current income tax deduction based on the future value of the gift to the charity. The income stream received may also receive favorable income tax treatment.

CGAs have many of the same benefits as a Charitable Remainder Trust without the set-up costs or ongoing need for administration. If you are willing to give up control of the investment management of your assets, a CGA may be a good choice for you.

Irrevocable Life Insurance Trusts

Many tax advisors and financial planners recommend and use Irrevocable Life Insurance Trusts (also referred to as ILITs or Wealth Replacement Trusts) to replace assets or property given to charity or to a Charitable Remainder Trust. An ILIT is created during the creator's lifetime, utilizing life insurance purchased on the life of the creator or the creator and her spouse as the primary asset of the trust. The increased cash flow derived from Charitable Remainder Trust planning (both the savings from the current income tax deduction as well as the increased income stream) can be used to fund the premium payments due on the life insurance. This technique can be extremely valuable when the donor's retirement plan assets are used as the primary charitable gift asset.

ILITs are also valuable planning tools to provide liquidity for the payment of estate taxes if family assets are primarily real estate investments or other business interests. Work closely with your legal, financial and tax professionals to determine if an ILIT is consistent with your goals.

Trust Administration

The administration of charitable trusts, private foundations, supporting organizations and irrevocable trusts should be performed by a professional trust administration company. Delegating this task to a family member, although less expensive in appearance, may have significantly greater risks due to the potential for mismanagement or the loss of valuable income and estate tax deductions. A professional administration company can provide the following benefits:

- Strict attention to all compliance and tax reporting issues
- Custody and sale of gifted assets
- Cost basis recorded for gifted assets
- Calculation of income tax charitable deduction
- Calculation of income tax charitable deduction
- Calculation of annual trust values to determine income beneficiary distributions

- Revaluation of trust assets and distributions based on added contributions
- Inventory of all trust assets, their fair market value and cost basis
- Record all trust transaction based on a four-tier accounting system
- Record all dividend, interest and principal payments
- Daily cash sweeps to taxable or tax-free money markets
- Coordination and payment of distributions to all income beneficiaries
- Preparation of final accounting at the termination of the trust
- Distribution of remaining trust assets to the appropriate beneficiaries

It is clear that wealth legacy is far more than "just our stuff." It is the passing of our values as well as our valuables. The methods and techniques we use to accomplish these goals are many and give us a number of options for creating the most appropriate methods to meet our particular needs. ⁂

chapter seven

Children: Blessings and Responsibilities

Children don't fit neatly into the The Confidence Continuum. They can come at any time during the course of our lives, so we've devoted a chapter to specifically discussing the concerns that arise when children arrive.

Once you've made the decision to have children, either your own biological children, through adoption or surrogacy, or in some cases, circumstance; there are a number of legal issues you need to consider for their well-being when you are not available to take care of them either due to disability or death.

PUT ON YOUR OWN MASK fIRST

Every parent should have, at a minimum, the core estate planning directives in place that authorize others to handle medical and financial matters for them when they are unable to do so due to disability or death. Otherwise, your children could be in jeopardy if no one is clearly authorized to withdraw funds, make payments and transact other financial matters during a period of the parent's mental incapacity or death. Chapter Four sets forth an explanation of the core directives and other planning tools that parents may consider for their own wealth protection for the benefit of their children—a greater wealth than money.

Selecting a Guardian

Beyond the parent's legal directives regarding their own health and financial needs are directives related specifically to the children. One of the toughest decisions a parent faces is the one about who will be the guardian for their minor children in the event of the parent's death. We have one friend that says the only way he got his wife to go to the lawyer to make their Will that name the guardians for their children was to threaten that the kids would probably end up with his mother if they didn't. That was enough to get her going. The truth is, if you don't state or memorialize your wishes regarding guardian of your children, there is no guarantee that the people you trust most are the ones who will be selected. This is just one decision that should not be left up to chance.

When considering who will be most appropriate as a guardian for your children think about those individuals that share your same ideals, beliefs and socio-economic background. You may be lucky enough to find this person in your family, either a parent or a sibling. If not, perhaps you have a close friend that you could count on for this purpose. We recommend you discuss your intentions with the desired guardian to make sure they are on the same page with you regarding this important decision. You may even be able to "exchange" the favor and agree to raise your guardian's children if the tables are ever turned. In all likelihood you may never have to rely on your guardian but it is never a good idea to leave this decision up to chance or the court system.

In some cases, parents never undertake estate planning designed to protect their children because they are unable to agree on a common guardian. Some planning is better than no planning—in order for your choice of guardian to prevail, all you have to do is live longer than your spouse! Sometimes this advice is enough to get people out of a stand-off and into their attorney's office to do their planning.

BEYOND NOMINATING THE GUARDIAN

In addition to selecting a guardian, you'll also discuss with your attorney when and how assets should be distributed to your children. If your children are minors, the answers are usually pretty obvious. A trust should be created for their benefit to permit someone to manage the money for the children while they are minors. You could decide that the assets earmarked for them in trust should be distributed to them outright or in increments upon attaining an age specified by you, such as 21, 25, 28 or some other reasonable age of maturity. The trust can terminate at that time and the assets distributed outright to the children.

Or, you might find that directing that the trust terminate at some point with an outright distribution of assets would not be in the best interests of your child—even if the "child" is now an adult, albeit perhaps a young adult. Once assets are distributed outright and outside the protections of the trust, they offer no protection for the assets or for your child. The type of protections we are talking about are spendthrift protection, divorce protection, catastrophic creditor and/or bankruptcy protection and catastrophic illness protection. Put another way, this is protection from the child himself and protection from the world. The *Trust Protection Spectrum*™ in Chapter Six illustrates how greater protections are available as you move from left to right on the spectrum regarding distribution of assets.

No matter how well we try to teach our children the importance of financial asset management, some kids will always have more of a tendency to spend than to save. If your child is a spender, a trust can provide spendthrift protection—either by limiting distributions to a particular formula or by placing a more responsible party—a professional or corporate trustee in charge of the assets. In addition, some children end up with drug, alcohol or other issues that prevent them from being a good candidate either for outright distributions or for money management responsibilities. And, if you have a special needs child, it should go without saying that they won't be in a position to manage their own assets if they lack legal capacity. In addition, if your child is eligible for government benefits, you wouldn't want an inheritance to cause them to lose their benefits. For more information on protecting children with disabilities, read *Special People, Special Planning —Creating a Safe Legal Haven for Families with Special Needs*. See *www.SpecialPeopleSpecialPlanning.com* and Chapter Ten for more information.

Divorce protection is important because your child may marry someone they ultimately don't stay married to. We say this is when in-laws become outlaws. Divorce rates still range around 50% in this country so your child has only a one in two chance of not being a victim of divorce. If you leave an inheritance to your child and that asset is co-mingled with the assets of a spouse, when the divorce papers are served, the likelihood is that 50% of that joint asset will belong to the "outlaw." Most families we counsel with are genuinely concerned about protecting inherited assets from divorce and understand that continuing to hold assets in trust may provide the best type of protection they are looking for.

It seems as if there is a lawsuit waiting around every corner. Statistics today indicate that on average each of us will be party to two lawsuits in our lifetime. If divorce is one, then that still leaves a possible additional lawsuit. This lawsuit may come in the form of an auto accident, business failure, professional malpractice or bankruptcy, just to name a few. If your child is found to be the at-fault party and there is a judgment entered against him, the party holding the judgment is going to be very interested in determining what assets he might have available to satisfy this judgment. If your child has inherited a substantial amount of money that is outside of the protections of a trust you created, these assets may be fair game for the judgment creditor. If your child ever finds himself in a situation where he needs to file bankruptcy, again, his inherited assets will likely become part of the bankruptcy process and used to satisfy outstanding creditor claims. Creditor protection is one of the easiest protections to provide for your child—we recommend you consider Lifetime Protective Trusts™ for all your children, regardless of their financial maturity.

If your child either is or becomes catastrophically ill, a trust can provide the protection and professional money management necessary to maintain governmental benefits. If your child currently has special needs and is or may be dependent upon governmental benefits, a special needs trust may need to be created to preserve these benefits. Entitlement programs such as Social Security Income (SSI) and Medicaid generally have both income and asset limitations. If you leave assets outright to your child, they may either become disqualified if they are already receiving benefits or may be unable to qualify for benefits if they need to in the future.

If you want to provide a safety net for a child that is not currently catastrophically ill but may need assistance in the future, a trust can provide a stand-by trustee so that your child's assets can continue to be managed for their benefit when they are no longer able to do so.

Transferring Your Wisdom — Passing On Your Values

In addition to providing protections for our children through the use of trusts, a trust can also be used to pass on family values. Any number of guidelines can be tied to a trust to ensure that your children benefit from your life experience. We know of one man whose son never worked while his father was alive. At the father's death, the son received a surprise—he would only be entitled to receive assets from the trust created for his benefit in an amount equal to that which he was able to earn. In the final analysis, the father was able to convey his heartfelt value regarding the importance of developing a work ethic.

Another family we know elected to place a restriction on the amount of money that could be withdrawn annually from the child's trust to encourage the child to be a productive member of society. The restrictions, however, were relaxed if the child (a girl) wanted to stay home and raise a family. In that event, the trust would match her pre-baby salary so that she could maintain her standard of living. Other families we know have built language into their trusts providing incentives for children to work in traditional low-paying jobs such as education and missionary work. Some have even included incentives for graduation from college, graduate school and for staying married. Think of all the things you would want to teach your child and then translate that into instructions to be included in your estate planning. It is the only way to ensure that your values will be passed down to your children.

Chapter Six—Wealth Legacy discusses more ways to pass on values in addition to your financial assets.

Generation Skipping Provisions — Creating a Lasting Legacy

Some families have enough wealth that they don't want all of it spent during the generation of their children. They want the family legacy to persist from generation to generation. These are called dynasty trusts and were popularized by families like the Kennedys and Rockefellers. However, you don't have to be ultra wealthy to want assets to remain in the family bloodline. Be advised that Uncle Sam may impose a generation skipping tax penalty for exceeding the lifetime generation skipping exemption. Discuss legacy planning with your legal professional to determine whether a dynasty trust will meet your family's needs.

ADOPTION

Some families will elect to adopt a child to either create or supplement the family they already have. Be sure to work with a reputable legal representative and well-known adoption sources so that your rights are protected. Adoption is a very serious step—it is generally easier to adopt someone than it is to unadopt them if you are later unhappy about your decision.

Step-parent adoptions are relatively common in our society today as we divorce and remarry. Be advised that a step-parent adoption brings with it all of the rights and responsibilities of a natural parent. Your child can inherit from you and your family as if they were naturally born into that family. On the other hand, if a parent is giving up parental rights it may also result in a termination of inheritance rights by the child from that parent and their family. These issues are important to consider whenever adoption is a possibility.

It is also becoming more common for grandparents to adopt their grandchildren. We know a couple who not only adopted their granddaughter, they also adopted their great granddaughter! Family circumstances may be such that the grandparents find themselves in a position of wanting or having to provide for their grandchildren and adoption is the most expedient way of creating the legal rights and obligations necessary to facilitate the maintenance of their family.

Same sex couples are often prevented from adopting children depending on their state statutes. Seek the advice of counsel if you are in a same sex relationship or committed unmarried relationship and want to pursue your adoption rights.

SURROGACY

Many couples today are opting for surrogacy arrangements—finding a host mother either to supply an egg; or an egg and a womb for the purpose of creating a child. Unique legal rights and responsibilities may arise, and a surrogacy arrangement should be done under the watchful supervision of competent legal counsel. You may remember some of the widely publicized surrogacy agreements gone bad where surrogate mothers changed their mind and ultimately prevailed in obtaining the return of their child. States may vary as well in their interpretation or acceptance of surrogacy arrangements.

THE IMPORTANCE OF PERSONAL INSTRUCTIONS

Regardless of the way your child(ren) became part of your family, protecting them is a number one priority. Every parent needs to have estate planning directives that clearly state their intentions regarding their children. Remember, state statutes create a plan for your children when you fail to do so. These default plans might not be what you would want for your child. Better to plan by design rather than by default—especially where your children are concerned.

In addition to your legal documents—a Will and/or a Living Trust along with appropriate ancillary documents—you'll want to leave personalized instructions for the care of your children.

Supplemental instructions are like baby sitter instructions. Remember the first time you left your child with the baby sitter? You didn't just walk out the door, hand over the child and say "good luck." Instead, you probably had several pages of instructions detailing everything that might possibly arise in the few hours that you planned to be gone. Everything from feeding, changing, diapering, games, television, bathing, toileting, bed times and bedtime stories. And then you left as many contact phone numbers as possible in case of an emergency or unexpected event. You also probably called home a number of times to check on how things were going. Yet many of us don't give as much thought to the types of instructions we would leave in the event we were to depart this world permanently with no hope of being contacted.

Consider creating a notebook for your children providing extensive details for each of them and providing all of the necessary information that will be needed to provide them with love and care consistent with what you would have provided if you were there personally. If done in a loose-leaf format, you can easily update your notebook as your children get older and their requirements change. Your children are always going to be your children, no matter how old they get and you will always want to provide instructions for their continued care.

Please read *A Matter of Trust—The Importance of Personal Instructions* for more information on how to supplement your legal instructions with important personal instructions. Visit *www.AMatterOfTrust.info* for more information.

Pets—Your Children Who Wear fur Coats

If you are like many women today, you may have opted not to have children, in the traditional sense. Instead, your children may have four legs and wear fur coats—either in the form of dogs, cats, horses or other furry friends.

Our pets are like our children and as a result you will want to include them in your estate plan. You may even want to create a trust for your pet—called a pet trust—that will last the test of time and provide for your pets if and when you are no longer able to do so personally; either through catastrophic event, disability or death. A pet trust can provide instructions for an Animal Care Panel™ or pet care guardian to provide the day-to-cay care for your pet as well as trustee instructions for the management and distribution of the assets. Even if you don't create a formal trust for your pets, make sure that you leave adequate financial resources for your pet's guardian to ensure they will always be properly cared for.

You may have a household that has both pets and kids. The same advice applies to you. You can't ever be sure that your family—your spouse or your children—will be willing and able to care for your pets if something happens to you. Be sure to provide adequate instructions to provide for your pets.

Bob and Mary had a long and happy marriage. They never had any two-legged children, but Bob especially loved his dog, Ziggy. Bob assumed that Mary would always take care of Ziggy if something happened to him. When Bob died and Mary later remarried, her new spouse was allergic to Ziggy and they determined they were unable to keep him. Ziggy ended up at a local animal shelter. Fortunately, Ziggy was rescued and adopted by a loving family, instead of the more likely scenario—euthanasia.

In addition to providing instructions for your pets as part of your estate planning, keep a notebook for your pets. The notebook should provide details for each of your pets including photos, medical history and information regarding care requirements, likes and dislikes. Your pet notebook should resemble the one you might prepare for two-legged children in the form of baby sitter instructions. *All My Children Wear Fur Coats—How to Leave a Legacy for your Pet* provides checklists and ideas on some of the details a good pet plan should have. Visit *www.LegacyForYourPet.com* for more information.

Our children, whether two-legged or four-legged deserve to be protected and require that we spend the time and energy to make sure they are properly provided for. ⁂

chapter Eight

L i f e   C r i s i s

N ot every phase of life will be predictable or without tragedy. There may be times when you may experience a life crisis: the loss of a loved one (family member, spouse or partner, child, friend or pet); a catastrophic illness or accident; financial reversal; sudden unemployment; natural disaster or some other unexpected event that wasn't envisioned as part of your overall life plan. A life crisis can be anything that doesn't fit nicely into what you had planned. However, if you plan ahead, even a crisis can be managed so that you come out on the other end with your head held high ready to start again.

NATURAL DISASTERS

It seems that natural disasters of all types—fires, hurricanes, tornadoes, mud slides, and flooding have become a common part of the evening news, especially in parts of the South or West. It also seems that every day someone, somewhere, and not necessarily outside of the United States, is experiencing a severe natural disaster.

Your best defense against any type of natural disaster is a plan. In much the same way as you've created an estate plan or a financial plan, it is important to have a natural disaster plan. If you need to leave your home on only a moment's notice, what will you absolutely, positively have to take with you?

If you have adequate liability insurance, your home and most of your personal property should be protected against loss. But consider the things that can't be easily replaced—things like pictures, family heirlooms, original art work, important original legal documents (birth certificates, passports, estate planning documents) and your pets. What kind of plan do you have for safeguarding these precious assets in the event of an emergency? The recent Gulf Coast hurricanes brought the nation's attention to the importance of having a disaster plan for family members and pets, leaving early rather than waiting for disaster to strike, and being constantly vigilant about being prepared.

Many legal and financial documents can be scanned electronically so that at least a copy is saved on the hard drive of your computer or on an easy-to-carry "jump drive." Digital photos can document your valuable items throughout your home for assistance in insurance claim recovery. Having an undetectable microchip imbedded in your pet can provide for easy identification in the event you are separated during an evacuation or time when you must leave your pets behind. (Note: More shelters are permitting owners to bring their pets. However, don't rely on a shelter to provide housing for your pets—figure out ahead of time where you will go, including how your pet will be provided for, and what you will do.) You can also place identification stickers on the outside of your home identifying pets inside and contact information in the event of emergency when you cannot be contacted or cannot take your pets with you—these are especially helpful if volunteers or firefighters are searching the area.

Keep irreplaceable items in a place where they can be easily removed and transported if you have the luxury of more time. This means planning ahead and thinking about what things are most important to you and having an evacuation plan.

Make sure family members have current contact numbers and information for cell phones, shelters or community services. This is especially crucial for out-of-state family members. Create a plan of action that your family can follow when your geographical area is hit. This might mean a plan to call a specified number at a specified time rather than having family frantically attempt to reach you.

From a financial perspective, you should have six (6) months of spending money in reserve—your emergency reserve. This may be the time that you need to get to the bank and turn some of that emergency money into cash. It may not be practical to think that you will be able to write a check or use a debit or credit card for purchases in the event of an emergency.

Obviously, not all natural disasters are going to provide you with the time you need to protect your valuables. For this reason, do what you can before the need arises. It may help alleviate your stress later on. For more information, you can visit the website for the American Red Cross *(www.redcross.org)* for more information and helpful advice.

fINANCIAL DISASTER

A financial disaster can arise in any number of ways. You could experience unmanageable debt, a divorce, the loss of your job, permanent disability where you are unable to work or the death of a spouse or partner, just to name a few. Having a financial disaster plan is going to be your best defense for these possible circumstances. This plan includes liquid assets in reserve, lines of credit or disability insurance described in prior chapters, especially Chapter Four regarding wealth protection. If all else fails, you may find bankruptcy is the best plan of action. It can halt complete financial devastation and allow you to recover your equilibrium.

Bankruptcy

Filing bankruptcy should be a last ditch effort to overcome any financial difficulty you may encounter. A bankruptcy on your credit record has lasting effects that can follow you for years. Bankruptcy is not an easy solution to years of poor spending habits or an unexpected financial turn in your life. Never contemplate bankruptcy lightly and only with the guidance of legal and financial professionals.

If bankruptcy is your only option, then you'll need good legal counsel. Beware of cut-rate legal services that offer a low, low price. Generally you get what you pay for and you're going to need good advice, not someone who is simply going to file the paperwork and leave you to your own devices. Your legal counsel should advise you which type of bankruptcy is right for your situation. In fact, state and federal rules may dictate which form of bankruptcy will be appropriate. Be advised that the federal bankruptcy rules have changed recently and what was true a few years ago may not be true today. Don't take legal advice regarding bankruptcy from your friends or well-meaning professionals who are not legal practitioners in this area. Bankruptcy law is a very specialized area of the law that requires year of practice to master. Just because a friend or acquaintance has been through the bankruptcy process doesn't mean that you are going to have the same experience. Every situation will be unique.

There are essentially two types of personal bankruptcy: "Chapter 7" and "Chapter 13" which refer to the chapter sections where the rules appear within the bankruptcy laws. The goal in a Chapter 7 bankruptcy is to liquidate assets in order to pay existing creditors and then discharge those debts that can't be paid. A Chapter 13 bankruptcy, on the other hand, doesn't require asset liquidation, but proposes a plan of repayment, generally over five (5) years. Each of the two types of personal bankruptcy has its own rules regarding which assets you can keep and those that may have to be sold. They also will determine which assets are exempt from the bankruptcy proceedings that you can keep—for example, your house or a car. The rules will also determine which debts can be discharged in bankruptcy. Some debts like taxes, student loans, alimony and child support payments are not eligible for discharge in bankruptcy.

Chapter 7 Bankruptcy

Chapter 7 bankruptcy is essentially a liquidation proceeding where the court will determine what property you will have to sell to pay your debts. The law provides that you can keep certain property, called exempt property. The federal law provides for certain exemptions and so does state law. Depending on the state you live in, you may have the option to choose between the federal exemptions or your state exemptions. Examples of possible exempt assets are your home or a portion of your home, your car, jewelry, tools of your trade, household goods and furnishings and in some cases, your retirement savings.

Any property that is not exempt would then be available to be sold to pay your creditors—hopefully in full, but at least in part. Debts that are unsecured, like credit card charges or revolving credit accounts that are not paid in full would then be discharged. Secured debts, like your home, car or furniture would likely be repossessed by the creditor and then sold with the sale proceeds going toward the payment of the debt. In most cases, the sale price is not sufficient to pay the total amount owed and the balance would then be discharged in the bankruptcy. If you were not in bankruptcy and an asset was repossessed and sold, the remaining amount owed could become a judgment lien against you that may still have to be paid.

Chapter 13 Bankruptcy

In a Chapter 13 bankruptcy, you are not required to sell your assets so that the proceeds can be used to pay your creditors. Instead, you enter into a plan of reorganization that gives you an opportunity to pay off your debts, either fully or partially, over a period of time. The time period can vary but it is usually a three (3) to five (5) year time period. The amount you pay is determined by what is left after your monthly living expenses. If you make all your payments timely and complete the plan successfully, the remaining unpaid debt will be discharged, with some exceptions.

Sometimes people elect a Chapter 13 bankruptcy to avoid the loss of their secured assets, like their home. Generally you have to continue to make your regularly scheduled payments along with an additional payment toward the amount you are overdue. If you complete this payment plan successfully, your mortgage will no longer be considered past due.

Which type of bankruptcy you choose will depend on a number of factors, not the least of which will be what you are trying to accomplish and the rules related to the different choices. Your circumstances may dictate which form of personal bankruptcy will be right for you.

As we've mentioned, bankruptcy should only be used as a last resort. Once you've filed bankruptcy your credit history will carry that notation for a period of ten (10) years. This means every time you try and obtain credit during that ten year period, the bankruptcy notation will appear. It may affect your ability to make periodic payments on other items such as insurance, as well. Some employers even check your credit history as an indicator of your personal character in determining whether to hire or promote you.

Ultimately, time and your good efforts to manage your spending and improve your credit will allow you to get credit again. It may be a long road—you may have to get secured credit cards and/or pay higher interest rates. Be advised, you can only file bankruptcy on a limited basis. The law will dictate how often you can resort to this option. It is not a solution for poor budgeting or bad spending habits. A bankruptcy is intended only as a solution of last resort.

Getting Divorced or Otherwise Starting Over

It would be our desire that you never have to read this section. Sadly, about 50% of marriages end in divorce. The statistics are more grim for people marrying for a second and third or more time. The importance of this section is that this is certainly a time of transition and one that will require some follow-up and follow-through on your part.

Making sure you have competent counsel is essential. The availability of Internet "do it yourself" marriage dissolutions and yellow-pages low cost divorce attorneys create an illusion that divorce is relatively simple. Nothing could be further from the truth even when the parting couple agrees to the property division, visitation of children and other details.

Remember, divorce is not just about ending a marriage. The resources and liabilities you take from the marriage become the foundation for your future—for better or worse. An essential part of wealth protection is understanding what you have, its value, and how to best protect it. An experienced domestic relations attorney knows the questions to ask and the legal impact of every decision you are asked to make. He or she has been through the process many, many times. If this is the end of your first marriage, you have zero experience with the divorce process and its pitfalls.

Don't make the mistake of thinking you will save money by doing things yourself. Don't think you can't afford an attorney either. Many domestic relations attorneys agree to payment plans to allow clients to pay for their services. In matters such as these, you can't afford not to at least consult an attorney. A financial advisor should also be part of your team if the assets in question are sizeable. In addition, there are credentialed financial divorce planners that may be able to help you make some of the difficult financial decisions. At a minimum, a financial advisor should be consulted about a post-divorce financial plan. Remember the statistics in Chapter One and remember The Confidence Continuum strata of wealth creation and wealth protection. Don't consign yourself to a life of anxiety and limitations imposed by hasty and uninformed decisions made during a time of emotional turmoil.

Chapter Nine gives guidance on selecting advisors. Read this for suggestions on how to find someone suited to your needs. One of the toughest things about divorce and your relationship with your lawyer is that in the end, it is still a divorce and rarely does anyone feel like they got what they wanted or deserved. The whole process seems to be one of compromise that is fueled by lots of emotional highs and lows. Take comfort in knowing that someday you'll be beyond the legalities of the divorce and in a position to start a new chapter in your life.

Divorce Issues

Some common themes that come up in a divorce context are certainly going to be the division of property or assets, the division of liabilities, alimony, child support, visitation, health insurance and life insurance. There will be additional issues depending on your particular situation but these tend to be the core themes that require a decision.

At the first hint of a divorce or legal separation, most domestic relations attorneys recommend that their potential client make copies of all financial papers regarding assets and liabilities, including copies of beneficiary designations, titles to real property and motor vehicles and insurance policies—including insurance riders for things like jewelry, furs and artwork. These should be kept in a safe place *outside* of the home where they are not accessible to the other spouse.

If the divorce becomes contentious, the other spouse can play hardball and make it difficult to gain access to information. This can also be a way to detect whether there have been expenditures or withdrawals from accounts as a means of depressing their values for negotiating purposes.

If you signed a prenuptial agreement prior to your marriage, many of these issues may have been "resolved." This is why it is so important to get good advice at the prenuptial stage when life is rosy and the relationship looks like it will last forever. Decisions that are made at the prenuptial stage can come back to haunt you now. Annette, the young fiancé, would probably regret her decision to waive alimony if she was no longer employable at a sufficient salary because she remained out of the workforce to raise children.

Division of Property

In many states, the starting point for division of property is that all property acquired during the marriage and owned jointly by the parties is considered to be marital property, subject to division at the time of divorce. Therefore, there are a couple of rules of thumb—if you don't want property to be treated as marital property, don't put your husband's name on it. In separate property states this should work very well but won't necessarily have the same effect in community property states.

There are eight community property states left in the nation—they are Arizona, California, Idaho, Louisiana, Nevada, New Mexico, Texas, Washington, and Wisconsin. In Alaska, spouses can sign an agreement making specific assets community property. The premise of community property is that all property acquired during the marriage, regardless of title, is deemed to be a marital asset. The net effect of this is when parties divorce that all property acquired during the marriage is subject to equitable division.

The following chart describes the differences between community property and separate property states.

Community Property	Separate Property
Money either spouse earns during marriage belongs to both spouses	Property owned by one spouse before marriage belongs to the one who owned the property
Things bought with money either spouse earns during marriage belongs to both spouses	Property given to just one spouse remains the property of that spouse, if not co-mingled
Separate property that has become so mixed with community property that it can't be identified belongs to both spouses	Property inherited by just one spouse remains the property of that spouse, if not co-mingled

The division of property in a divorce requires making a list of all the assets and their values. Then the trading begins. The goal is for each party to walk away with their reasonable fair share of the pie. This is generally one of the hardest parts of the divorce process. A lot of emotions can come into play here because of emotional attachments to our "stuff" as well as feelings of having contributed more or less to the acquisition of certain assets.

Be aware that "value" is a relative concept. Some asset values can be manipulated or "obscured" to tilt the balance in favor of one of the spouses. This is particularly true if that spouse is self-employed or a business owner. Retirement accounts are another resource that can require special valuation.

It is never a good idea to accept values on such assets without professional scrutiny. Money makes people do funny things. Even the most trust-worthy spouse can justify all sorts of shenanigans to retain an asset to the detriment of the other spouse during a divorce.

There will usually be some division of the real property and/or your home. If there are minor children, you may be permitted to keep the home until the youngest child has attained the age of 18. Important considerations are going to be how you are going to maintain the house on your own, both financially and mechanically and whether this is something you really want to do. Again, a financial planner can assist in this decision-making process. Be sure to consider the services of a planner who is familiar with the specific issues presented in the divorce process. Some resources for certified divorce planners are given in Chapter Ten.

Division of Liabilities

Many couples, especially if they haven't been married very long, seem to have more debt than assets. It can be a painful part of leaving a relationship when it feels like all you are getting is the responsibility for debt. In some property settlements, it seems like one spouse ended up with all the assets, while the other ended up with the lion's share of the debt—the old "she got the goldmine, I got the shaft" scenario, although the shoe may be on the other foot. There is a caution here. Beware of the amount of debt that you accumulate—too much and it may be the only thing there is to divide in the event of a divorce. If you've learned your budgeting and savings lessons well, then your debt should be at manageable levels and not represent the biggest portion of your financial portfolio.

One little known fact is that despite what your marital settlement agreement says about who is going to be responsible for what debt—your contract with the credit card company generally trumps any marital settlement agreement. If you are jointly obligated on a debt contract and your former husband assumes responsibility as part of your divorce and then defaults in his payments, it is likely that the credit card company will come after you to pay it off. You incurred the debt jointly, you signed the credit card agreement jointly, and the credit card company cares little for what the court decided about who is responsible for the debt. If your spouse is the defaulting party, it may be far more costly for you to try and pursue enforcement of this provision of your marital settlement agreement than it would be for you to simply pay the debt.

Mary Ann learned this lesson the hard way. She and Jason were married for 20 years. They had grown apart emotionally and when Jason asked for a divorce, Mary Ann agreed. There was no acrimony between them. They were friends but no longer "in love." They didn't see the need of each getting a lawyer since they weren't fighting over anything. They didn't want to pay an attorney when they were in agreement about how their assets would be divided.

They downloaded some dissolution papers from a "do it yourself" divorce website on the Internet. They dutifully filled in the blanks on the forms. In fact, they were quite proud about they way they resolved how Mary Ann would be reimbursed by Jason for some money her father had loaned her prior to her marriage. She had given the money to Jason to start a business. They agreed that Jason would be responsible for the credit card balances which roughly equaled the sum Mary Ann had given Jason.

The divorce was finalized for a modest cost of $250.00—the cost of the downloaded forms and court filing fees. Mary Ann and Jason went their separate ways. Six years later, Mary Ann started to receive collection notices from the credit companies listed on the settlement agreement. It turns out that Jason's business was experiencing a severe downturn and he was defaulting on these and other accounts.

Long story short, the settlement agreement never specified what "being responsible for" the debts actually meant. Jason was paying only the minimum amount required each month. He did not close the accounts because he and Mary Ann never thought to do this. The interest on the accounts ballooned the balances to approximately $40,000.00. Mary Ann never notified the credit company that she was no longer responsible for the accounts and had not insisted that Jason close the accounts as part of the settlement.

Jason ultimately filed for bankruptcy which left Mary Ann as the only party left who was responsible and collectable under the credit contract. Her protests that these debts were Jason's because they agreed to this arrangement in the property settlement fell on deaf ears. She remained fully liable for their payment.

The lesson here is: establish your own credit. Avoid jointly obligating yourself on your spouse's or partner's credit cards and vice versa. Be just as careful authorizing a spouse or others as authorized users. Consult a financial advisor regarding the impact closing an account might have on your credit score. Consult an attorney who can help you look at all angles when negotiating a property settlement. In Mary Ann's case, a few extra dollars spent on a consultation with an attorney would have saved over $40,000.00 in unpaid debt.

Another issue that should be addressed in a marital settlement agreement is the transfer of real property. We've seen plenty of marital settlement agreements that state that one party or the other is obligated to sign a deed conveying their interest in the marital property or some other jointly owned property and then the divorce is over and no one has ever actually signed the required deeds. Enforcing this later can be expensive and time consuming, if not fruitless. Jenna is still trying to locate her former husband 20 years after their divorce to get him to sign a deed that should have been signed at the time of divorce. She wants to refinance her home and in the process discovered that his name was still on the deed. Now she has to find him, then she has to convince him to sign the deed conveying his interest to her. This effort is costing her money in the form of a private detective, attorney's fees and process server fees. All of this could have been avoided if the required documents were executed as part of the divorce rather than at some unspecified time thereafter.

Life Insurance

Life insurance is another issue that can be very important in a divorce situation, especially if there are minor or disabled children of the marriage that will require care in the event the primary caregiver dies or in the event the non-custodial parent dies and the stream of child support payments no longer exists. Most marital settlement agreements we've seen don't address this very important issue sufficiently. Make sure it is clear how much insurance is going to be provided, who will be the owner of the policy, who is to pay the premiums, who the beneficiaries are and whether or not you are going to be entitled to notice from the insurance company if there is a change to the policy. It is generally recommended that if the life insurance is going to be on the life of your spouse that you own the policy so that you can control the beneficiary designation. Otherwise, if your spouse owns the policy, the beneficiary designation should be irrevocable so that it can't be changed without your knowledge. You'll also want some evidence that the premium payments are being made on a consistent basis and that the policy is maintained in full force and effect. The best way to do this is to be the owner and to require that the payments be made to you so that you can pay the premium or that proof of payment is provided prior to the termination of the policy. This is probably one of the most important issues of your marital settlement agreement because it is the financial pivot point upon which your alimony and child support payments rest— translated as, the ongoing well-being of you and your children.

We don't mean to minimize the importance of child support payments but child support is generally dictated by state statute and the prevailing state child support guidelines. In some states you may be able to reach an agreed upon child support payment but that would not be the norm. Generally child support is based upon a formula calculated by the incomes of both the husband and the wife and the number of children. As a parent you do not have the right to waive your child's entitlement to child support. If you have a disabled child, you may be entitled to child support payments beyond the normal age of majority.

Child Support

We've heard a number of mothers say over the years that if their former husband would just leave them and their child(ren) alone that they would not be interested in child support. Sadly, this is not a right that a mother or parent has the ability to waive. The entitlement to support belongs to the child. This means that children over the age of 18 may have a right to enforce back child support payments that might not have been made timely during their childhood.

Enforcing child support can be a full-time job if your former spouse is not punctual in his payments. Many states today have "dead-beat" dad programs to assist in the collection process, but many don't. Some people always receive their child support as required and others receive little or none of the court ordered support. Some women find it easier and more peaceful not to continuously pursue their legal remedies in the courts. This may be especially true if your former spouse lives in another state and not in the home state of the child.

Along with the idea of child support naturally comes visitation. Visitation is one of the most hotly contested issues in a divorce and can cause issues for years to come. Your divorce attorney will advise you about your options. An unstructured visitation schedule might be an option if the relationship between you and your former spouse is cordial. Hopefully, both parents will have lots of opportunities to spend time with their child(ren) and not have to squabble over birthdays, holidays, vacations and special events. In other cases, where the relationship is anything but cordial, visitation can be extremely structured with family turmoil over missed visitation days or the insistence that the rules be followed to the absolute letter. In some cases, families can spend tens of thousands of dollars in court over visitation rights. One friend has had a very contentious child support challenge that has continued for a number of years. All is calm as of this writing but there are always thunder clouds on the horizon—inevitably, there will be no true peace until the child attains the age of majority.

Regardless of the visitation structure, be sure to get a clear statement from your divorce attorney and include instructions in your divorce agreement about how the visitation schedule will be enforced, and at whose cost, if it is violated. One parent can thumb their nose at an agreement if they know the other parent can't afford to hire counsel to enforce it.

The visitation equation can be further complicated if your former spouse lives in another state and your child(ren) must travel in order to meet the child visitation guidelines. In our interstate travels, we've both seen many unaccompanied children traveling to meet a parent in another state. We've also seen parents that travel with their child(ren) and then either make a vacation of it themselves or turn around and return home.

Estate Planning Issues

After a divorce, it is going to be important to update your estate planning and/or do it for the first time if you've neglected this item thus far in your life. Now that your spouse is not the natural object of your affection and will not be your heir at law, it is imperative that you provide for the protection of your children.

Your estate planning documents need to reflect your revised choice for agent under your Financial Power of Attorney for financial decision making. You'll also want to revise your choice for healthcare surrogate under your Healthcare Power of Attorney and Living Will. In addition, you will want to include trust provisions in your Will or Living Trust for the benefit and protection of your minor children. If you die and they inherit your estate, you'll want to make sure they have professional money management either indefinitely or until they reach an age of maturity.

With respect to guardians, you'll want to name an alternate guardian in the event their father is unable or unwilling to act as guardian for the kids. This is an issue that may come as a surprise to some of you. As long as their father is living he will be their natural guardian. We've had many mothers distress over this situation because they don't feel comfortable having their former husband as the guardian for the children. There really isn't much you can do in this situation because as the biological parent, their rights are still intact and they will be the court's first choice for the children. In one unbelievable case we know of, the mother fought for years with her former husband over custody of their child. She truly felt he was not an appropriate role model for the child. She was ultimately successful in gaining full-time residential custody of her son only to take her own life and put her child right back into the hands of the one person she didn't want to have him. It was a very sad ending to a desperate situation. To add salt to the family's wounds, their daughter died without a Will and the former husband was also awarded the right to administer his former wife's estate and take possession of all of the property—presumably for the benefit of the child. A proper estate plan could not have avoided the guardianship issue but could have prevented the former spouse from controlling the assets.

Control of the assets is a common concern expressed to us by our female clients after a divorce. Most are adamant that no matter what happens, they don't want their former husband to control any assets on behalf of the children. This issue is easily rectified with proper planning. You can name whomever you like to administer your estate and preserve the estate assets for the benefit and protection of the children.

Asset Ownership and Beneficiary Designations

One thing you definitely need to do after a divorce is to double check all of your assets for proper ownership and proper beneficiary designations. Get a legal professional to help you if you are unsure of what you are doing. Title to all of your assets should be consistent with your estate plan. If you have a Will, everything should be owned in your individual name. If your asset is a beneficiary designation type of asset like an insurance policy or retirement plan, make sure that designation is consistent with your plan. For Will based plans, either the trustee of the trust created in your Will should be named or your estate. If you've created a Living Trust, your assets should be owned in the name of the trust and for beneficiary assets, your trust should be named as the primary beneficiary.

We want to caution you against ever naming your minor children as beneficiaries. Children under the age of 18 are not legally entitled to contract or own assets. If you name a minor child as your beneficiary, there is a great likelihood that a guardianship will have to be established for the child's benefit until they reach age 18. In addition, you may not want assets delivered to your child at age 18. We don't know of many 18 year olds that would spend and invest money wisely. The insurance industry has indicated that it doesn't matter how much a person receives or how old they are when they receive it, the money is generally gone in nine to 18 months. This is not the result you want for your child. There was one case reported in the Orlando papers about a young girl who had received a $25,000 inheritance outright. Her idea of a proper investment was a new car and party for her friends. She ended up on drugs and ultimately died. Until then she had been a straight "A" student and a seemingly responsible young adult. Don't take the chance that your teen or young adult is not responsible enough to manage money—it is your responsibility as a parent to ensure that your child is protected.

Divorce presents a number of transitional opportunities, both financial and legal. The responsibility for making sure that you are adequately protected rests squarely on your shoulders. Employ the assistance of professionals to help you through this difficult time and help set you on a revised course for a successful future.

Other Life Disasters

The Loss of a Loved One

The loss of a spouse, child, loved one or pet can be one of the most emotionally devastating disasters you will ever experience. Sadly, death is a part of life and eventually we all experience its pain. There is no way to avoid it, only ways to cope with our loss.

If you have recently experienced the loss of a loved one, seek counseling or a support group to help you through the grieving experience. Grieving is a fairly predictable process that has stages that must be processed and experienced until you reach acceptance and have the ability to grow again. You should not be expected to go through this process alone, nor do you have to. There are many people that are experiencing a similar pain and sharing their experience may help you. If you are not comfortable in a group, there are on-line chat rooms as another form of support. You may find that your local community or church offers assistance with the grieving process. In Orlando, there is the New Hope Center for Grieving Children to assist families and children with the loss of a loved one. For people who have lost a pet, the Association for Pet Loss and Bereavement *(www.aplb.org)* or the Rainbow Bridge *(www.rainbow-bridge.com)* can be a source of comfort.

The Loss of Your Job

The loss of you job can also be devastating. You may find yourself out of your element and wondering where you are going to go next. This can be a challenge or an opportunity. Look at it as an opportunity to do something different, improve your skills, change careers, change locations, and experience growth. Many communities provide skill assessment and training programs to assist down-sized workers in locating employment in the same or other fields. If this happens to you, try not to panic, do take stock of your strengths and talents and regroup in any way that feels right for you. There is another opportunity around the next corner—no situation is ever hopeless, especially if you have a financial emergency plan in place. Sometimes we need to be forced into change to experience its benefits. If you can't or don't want to go it alone, there are professional counselors trained to help you make the adjustment.

If you have been let go from your position, you may qualify for unemployment benefits and you should go to the local unemployment office and make application. These benefits may help keep you afloat while you are looking for your next opportunity.

If your job search takes longer than expected, you may have to consider more radical ways to come up with income, such as accessing a home equity line of credit, borrowing against the cash value in a life insurance policy, borrowing from family or friends, or withdrawing money from your tax-deferred retirement account. Each alternative has its drawbacks, but you'll want to be particularly careful with retirement accounts because you may incur fees and penalties that could increase your income tax liability at the end of the year. Some retirement plans offer an option to borrow money rather than actually withdrawing it and suffering penalties. You will, however, want to pay that money back as soon as you are able.

Next, take stock of your strengths and talents and update (or create) your resume. If you need help, there are lots of online and community resources for this purpose. Then, tell everyone you know what you are looking for and what you have to offer. Word of mouth is one of the best ways to find the type of employment you are looking for. Our best team members came to us by word of mouth—we wouldn't miss that job search opportunity for anything. Your local community colleges often provide job search services that you can take advantage of as well.

The Loss of Your Health

Your health is one of your most valuable assets. If you have your health, everything else can deteriorate and you can still survive. First and foremost, manage your health early on and you may avoid serious health conditions in the first place. Eat well, exercise daily, don't smoke, drink in moderation and get plenty of sleep. We sound like your mother or a doctor but it's just good common sense. If you are not doing these things, then you run a higher than average risk of serious health problems in the future. At any age before 65, you are more likely to be disabled (meaning at least 90 days out of work) than you are to die prematurely.

If you do suffer a catastrophic health issue or accident, where do you go from there? If you have health insurance, your medical expenses should be paid for. If you've heeded the advice of your financial advisor, you may have short and/or long-term disability insurance to provide for your living expenses. Many policies provide for as much as 60% of your salary, generally on a tax- free basis. Disability benefits can go a long way to keeping you financially sound while you recover from your illness. Some employers offer disability insurance as a job benefit. It's always a good idea to take advantage of these benefits but be advised that if you leave that employer your policy probably is not portable and you may be prevented from obtaining an individual policy in the future. Investigate all your options.

If you don't have disability insurance and you've worked and paid into the Social Security system, you may be eligible for Social Security Disability Income (SSDI). This is a government disability benefit for people with long-term illness that are unable to return to work for more than a year. Most people are denied on their first application, so work with a qualified legal professional in this area to improve your chances of success. If you do qualify, your lifestyle is bound to suffer. It is unlikely your monthly benefit will meet all of your needs and you may need to make other financial adjustments. If you can't qualify for SSDI, your only other government benefit option may be Social Security Income (SSI) that will pay a low monthly income for food, clothing and shelter. These are poverty wages and require that you qualify from both an income and asset standpoint. The income limitation changes on a regular basis and the asset limit is around $2,000. As you can see, you really need to be indigent to qualify for SSI.

More About Social Security Disability Income and Supplemental Security Income

The Social Security Administration (SSA) has jurisdiction to determine a worker's eligibility for disability income under its Social Security Disability Income (SSDI) and Supplemental Security Income (SSI) programs. These programs require medical proof of conditions that prevent a person from engaging in "*sustained remunerative employment,*" a term defined by federal law. Benefits under both programs are normally referred to as "permanent and total" disability although the SSA does have the authority to grant disability benefits for closed periods that are not permanent. In other words, "permanent" can encompass long term disability that isn't permanent in the normal use of the word.

SSDI is available to workers who 1.) have made the requisite contributions into the social security fund via the FICA contributions from the worker and her employer over a specified minimum time frame and 2.) can prove they have the requisite level of medical and/or mental disability that precludes sustained remunerative employment.

The contributions over the specified time frame determine whether a person has "insurable status" to participate in this program. If the worker was employed in the private sector for the specified period of time and contributed into the SSA fund, she will have insurable status. She can apply for disability benefits if her medical condition causes a disability that prevents her from working for at least 5 months with the expectation that the disability will continue for at least 12 months.

SSDI benefits are not based on financial need and there is no review of a person's net worth or financial factors. However, if the applicant's combined income from SSDI and another program, such as worker's compensation, exceed specified thresholds, an offset of benefits will occur.

If you can't qualify for SSDI because you did not have sufficient qualifying earnings paid into the SSA system, you might be eligible for SSI benefits. SSI pays a low monthly benefit for food, clothing and shelter. These are subsistence level benefits tied to the national poverty level. You must qualify from both an income and asset standpoint as well as the same disability standard applied to SSDI applicants. The financial limits makes the SSI program what is called a "needs based" benefit program. The income limitation changes on a regular basis and the asset limit is around $2,000. As you can see, you really need to be indigent to qualify for SSI.,

Although the standard for disability for both programs is the same, the programs differ in important ways in terms of the amount of the benefit and whether the applicant can own other assets. Many applications are denied at the first and second paper-review levels, so work with a qualified legal professional in this area to improve your chances of success. Attorney fees are paid on a contingency basis which means the attorney cannot be paid until she succeeds with your claim for benefits. SSA further limits attorney fees to no more than 25% of accrued benefits.

If you do qualify for benefits your lifestyle is bound to suffer. It is unlikely your monthly benefit will meet all of your needs and you may need to make other financial adjustments.

This explanation is a very brief summary of the programs. If you need to consider whether you are eligible for one of these programs, you should consult with an advisor who is experienced with these programs. Chapter Ten lists resources and includes the contact information for The National Association of Social Security Claimant Representatives. These are attorneys who are familiar with SSA rules.

Cash Value or Settlements Of Life Insurance

Another option for raising cash in the event of a life threatening catastrophic illness may be through an existing life insurance policy. If you have a life insurance policy that has accumulated cash value over the years, you can borrow against it. You must then pay back the borrowed amount. If you don't, the amount owed plus interest is subtracted from the death benefit. Or, you may want to consider surrendering your policy and getting a check for the cash value. The big downside here is that you will no longer have the policy and the larger death benefit that may be crucial for the protection of your family.

You may also have a life insurance policy that includes an accelerated benefits rider. If so, the accelerated benefit can be used if you have one year or less to live. The insurance company will pay a portion of the death benefit to you while you are still living. The portion is usually 25 percent, up to a certain maximum dollar amount. At your death, the insurance company will pay the balance of the death benefit to your beneficiary. There may be a charge for this benefit to cover administrative costs.

Another option is a viatical settlement or life settlement. This is a financial transaction whereby you, as the owner of a life insurance policy, sells the policy for cash while you're still living. The new owner, typically a viatical settlement or life settlement broker, takes over your premium payments and becomes the beneficiary of the policy. Companies that offer viaticals and life settlements may pay up to 60 percent of the face value of the policy, with the amount they pay based largely on the health and age of the insured. Work only with qualified professionals in the area of viatical and life settlements.

If life insurance is an important part of your financial plan, you won't want to change its character without careful consideration and consultation with your trusted advisors.

There are a number of disability insurance programs that you could consider. All are best viewed through the eyes of an insurance professional who can help you sort of the various bells and whistles and find a plan that will best meet your needs and budget. You may have the opportunity to have a disability plan through your employer or you may have to purchase a private disability plan on your own. Either way, disability protection is your best defense in the event of an unexpected illness or accident.

Other Options

There can be numerous other options that might come into play to help ease financial strain caused by the loss of a job or the loss of your health or other factors. For instance, veterans or surviving spouses of veterans may be eligible for on-going or one-time assistance from the Veterans Administration (VA). Many states have "homestead exemption" credits on real estate taxes for homeowners who are disabled and with limited income plus energy assistance programs that can help you free up funds. Reverse mortgages for homeowners can be an option to release the equity in a home. Unfortunately, there is no easy way to find out about potential programs to which you may be entitled. Few legal or financial advisors or social workers will be familiar with all such programs or financial strategies. Each might have a little view of the larger picture. Therefore, you will need to persevere and ask questions of everyone who might be in a similar situation.

We hope you never find yourself relying on the advice in this chapter. If you've taken our advice in previous chapters, hopefully this one won't ever be necessary. Have a plan, plan A and plan B if something prevents you from plan A; then work your alternate plan. No one ever planned to fail, they simply failed to plan.

As news headlines show again and again, life does go on after devastating natural disasters or personal tragedies. You are more likely to weather a crisis effectively if you have financial and legal protections in place before the crisis strikes. With or without such protections, you can always start over with the steps outlined in Chapter Three—Wealth Creation. You might have been knocked back a few steps but you can get up, dust yourself off, and get back on The Confidence Continuum toward independence. ✶

chapter nine

Trusted Advisors

We've talked at some length about the importance of building a trusted advisor team consisting of an estate planning/legal practitioner, financial advisor and certified public accountant (CPA). In this chapter we want to explore this topic further and give you some guidance on interviewing and selecting these individuals or other professionals.

As a preface to the discussion on selecting a professional team, let's explore one last time why a team is so important. We are frequently asked, "Why do I need a professional team? Can't I create my own financial and estate plans?" Our overwhelming response is, "You can try." Many have. Everyone already has a financial and estate plan, whether they know it or not. It might be the helter-skelter way you maintain your financial life or it might be your state's default plan for estate planning issues.

For some individuals, balancing their check books, paying their bills and owning assets jointly with a spouse or family member is the closet they ever come to a financial and estate plan. However, if you ask, "Does a 'do-it-myself' plan work for me and/or my family?" and you answer, "No," then you have made progress in recognizing that the financial and estate planning rules and laws are complex and you should seriously consider the guidance and advice of a professional. It pays to select your trusted advisors with care, since you will not survive financially or perhaps, literally, and your loved ones will live with the results.

Your trusted advisor team has spent thousands of dollars and years of time learning how to analyze problems and distinguish the simple from the complex. Finding a simple solution to a complex problem has as much value as unraveling a complex situation that may appear simple. Professionals add value to their services by their knowledge, skill and wisdom, continuing education, independent perspective and willingness to take responsibility for the results.

At this point, it should be abundantly clear that preparing and implementing your financial and estate plan is not an endeavor we recommend you should do yourself. You should only work with knowledgeable professionals who have an expertise in these areas and who encourage you to provide detailed personal information and instructions.

Specialization is becoming the norm. Everyone seems to have a niche area that they are concentrating their practice in. Beware of advisors who claim to "do it all." These are individuals we refer to as threshold practitioners because they will take any live body that can cross their threshold as a client. These are not the people that you are looking for. Instead, seek out those individuals whose area of concentration or expertise is consistent with your own needs. There are some financial advisors that primarily work with women. Others prefer to work with young families, business owners, or retirees. Some CPAs only want to work with small business owners, others only with individuals. Lawyers certainly run the gamut with their areas of expertise as well.

Family law attorneys specialize in divorce, child custody and other family law matters. Medical malpractice attorneys work in the area of seeking redress for injuries caused by medical personnel. If you are buying a home, you would utilize the services of a real estate attorney. In order to create an effective estate plan, you'll want a practitioner with a high degree of specialized knowledge and expertise. A general practice attorney won't have the breadth of knowledge necessary to provide comprehensive planning services or the ability to keep pace with future estate planning law changes.

SELECTING YOUR TEAM

Selecting the right team of advisors for you means doing your homework—educating yourself, defining your needs, learning to value professional services and seeking guidance in the selection of a qualified individual. The success of your financial and estate plans revolve around your relationship with your team of trusted advisors.

Unfortunately, there are many businesses and salespeople masquerading as financial and estate planning professionals. Ultimately their goal is to sell you something—to complete a "transaction" rather than truly develop a life-long relationship. Beware of advisors that are interested only in today's sale. Instead, seek individuals that have a well-defined process with specific steps that illustrate how they are going to help you create your plan and then keep it updated in the future. What is their process for staying in touch with you after you create your plan? Financial advisors will generally meet with their clients on a semi-annual or more frequent basis. You'll meet with your tax professional at least annually as you prepare your tax returns. And, you'll want to meet with your estate planning attorney not less than every two years to make sure your estate plan remains relevant to your family, financial and legal situation.

Selecting a Financial Advisor

What are you looking for in a qualified financial advisor? Do you want to work with a man, a woman, or with a team of professionals? Should they be young or have years of experience? What educational or professional qualifications are important to you?

Becoming a financial advisor and holding oneself out to the community as a financial advisor or financial consultant is a relatively easy process. Some financial practitioners have completed nothing more than a 40 hour insurance course that permits them to sell life and health insurance products. Others will have the licensure to also sell variable annuities. Still others will have taken courses of advanced study and may hold licenses such as a Series 63, Series 6 or Series 7, which allow them to sell certain financial products, like mutual funds, stocks and bonds. Serious professionals may obtain a Certified Financial Professional (CFP), Certified Financial Advisor (CFA), Certified Senior Advisor (CSA), Chartered Life Underwriter (CLU) or Chartered Financial Consultant (ChFC) designation, just to name a few. Be sure and ask your prospective advisor to explain these designations to you and to demonstrate the type of educational and practice requirements necessary to qualify. Most of these designations also require ongoing continuing education to keep the license current. If your advisor holds only a limited license, they will be limited in their ability to provide guidance and financial products. Ascertain how many years your prospective advisor has in the business and whether they take their own advice and have successful financial plans in place for themselves and their families.

Financial advisors charge for their services in a variety of ways. Some only work on commission which means they need to sell you something in order to get paid. Others work on a fee for service basis which means they may charge you a flat fee or percentage rate fee based on the value of your assets for the services they provide. Some advisors do both—charge a fee and work on a commission basis. Make sure you understand how your financial professional gets paid so you can add that to your evaluative process. There is no one right way for a financial advisor to get paid. Just know that in order to continue to want to provide service to you, there has to be some financial payoff for them. They aren't in the business of providing financial advice or financial products for free.

Some financial advisors will work for big companies where they may be required to sell only the services offered by that company. Others may be more independent and have flexibility in the types and quality of services they can offer. Some advisors will work in large offices with a number of other advisors, some will work in smaller independent offices and some may work from their homes. Just make sure you feel comfortable with their work-life arrangement as it may dictate where they meet with you to discuss your financial concerns. Some advisors are willing to meet with you in your home, at their office or at an alternate office or business location. It is not unusual for us to make our offices available to financial advisors that want to meet their clients there. If you are not comfortable having your financial advisor come to your home, suggest an alternate office or public location. A library may be a good choice if you don't have any other options.

Selecting a Tax Professional

In addition to a qualified financial advisor, you'll also want to have a tax professional on your team of advisors. The job of the tax professional is to provide you with advice related to the preparation of your annual tax return, as well as tax deferral and tax minimization techniques. If you are a small business owner, your tax professional should be providing guidance with regard to your business interests as well. Some tax professionals also provide bookkeeping services for individuals or businesses.

A tax professional doesn't have to be a Certified Public Accountant (CPA), but many are. A CPA has completed an educational course of study—usually four or more years in college and have passed a comprehensive examination that is extremely difficult. Others are Enrolled Agents (EA) which means they are registered with the Internal Revenue Service for the purpose of providing tax advice. Still others have taken courses from local tax preparation companies like H&R Block for the purpose of providing tax preparation services. We suggest you consider a CPA or Enrolled Agent for your tax preparation and advice needs. Ask your tax professional what their annual continuing education requirements are, what their area of specialization is and whether they are taking on new clients that meet your qualifications and needs.

Tax professionals usually charge on an hourly or flat fee basis. Make sure you understand what and how you will be charged so there are no surprises. It's a good idea to sign an engagement letter outlining the services they will provide and they manner in which they intend to bill for these services.

Selecting an Attorney

Attorneys are known by many different names, such as lawyer, counselor or counsellor, solicitor and advocate. Attorneys are required to obtain extensive educational training in order to be prepared and able to represent a client. To qualify to practice law, attorneys must first have an undergraduate degree and then earn a law degree—referred to as a Juris Doctor or J.D.—and then pass a state bar examination and commit to pursuing continuing legal education for the duration of their legal career.

Attorneys are subject to codes of ethical conduct and professional responsibility imposed by their state bar associations. Generally, the profession as a whole self-monitors its members. Attorneys can be sole practitioners, members of small firms or members of large firms. An attorney can be an associate, of counsel or a partner. Attorneys can be general practitioners or attorneys can specialize in a particular area of the law. You should seek an attorney who concentrates his or her practice in estate planning with specific expertise in trust planning.

Attorneys can be plaintiff oriented or defense oriented. They can be trial attorneys, called litigators, with a practice that focuses on trial work, or they can be transactional lawyers who concentrate on some of the non-litigation aspects of the law, such as corporate, real estate or estate planning. Then, there are attorneys who refer to themselves as "relationship oriented" attorneys because they are not merely interested in a client for a single transactional event, but desire an ongoing mutually rewarding and beneficial relationship with their clients.

Selecting an attorney will depend on many different factors—not the least of which is the purpose for which you are interviewing attorneys in the first place. It is important to think about attorneys in the same context as doctors. You wouldn't hire your family practitioner or gynecologist to conduct brain surgery, despite the fact they have the same underlying educational foundation. Additional training and years of specialized experience are determining factors in selecting the right professional for your legal needs.

Some attorneys are "board certified." Board certification is a voluntary designation program for attorneys. Certification requirements vary depending on your state and the area in which the attorney is seeking certification. Certification often requires additional continuing legal education requirements and may require the applicant to pass a certification examination. There may be additional requirements: that the attorney practice in the area of specialty for a number of years; devote a required percentage of his or her practice to the specialty area; handle a variety of matters in the area to demonstrate experience and involvement; attend ongoing continuing education; obtain favorable evaluations by fellow lawyers and judges; and pass a written examination.

Board certification will give you some indication of the attorney's competence in the area for which you are seeking legal advice. This is not to imply that attorneys who are not board certified do not have high levels of competence. Many highly qualified attorneys have chosen for personal or professional reasons not to seek board certification. It does not in any way diminish their qualification or commitment to excellence in their selected practice area.

It is important to understand the fees and billing arrangement before you get a bill from your attorney. Attorneys' fees can vary dramatically depending on the nature and scope of the legal services provided. The scope of the representation is an understanding as to what the attorney will do (or not do), how long it will take, what the attorney will not do without further authorization, what the client's goals are, and so forth. Financial arrangements should be as clear as possible, unless doing so would take longer than whatever it is the attorney is being retained to do. Even then, the maxim is to "put it in writing."

Some attorneys provide services on a flat-fee or quoted-fee basis while others provide services based on an hourly calculation, which becomes a function of the attorney's (and his or her staff's) hourly billing rate multiplied by the number of hours expended on your behalf. If you have legal needs of an ongoing nature, will the attorney agree to a retainer fee agreement where you pay a fixed fee each month for services? Are costs included in the quoted fee or will they be in addition to any quoted amounts? Are there any other add-ons, like legal research fees, paralegal costs, long distance phone charges or facsimile and copy charges?

There are a number of factors that may enter into the calculation of attorneys' fees. Some attorneys, like personal injury attorneys or workers' compensation attorneys, charge on a contingency basis or a percentage of the recovery obtained on your behalf. Others may charge on an hourly basis or on a project basis.

Higher hourly fees generally coincide with a lawyer's experience and/or geographic location. For example, an attorney in Los Angeles, Chicago, New York City or Washington, D.C., is likely to charge a higher hourly rate than a comparable attorney in a smaller city. Likewise, the size of the firm may dictate higher hourly rates for both partners and associates than a smaller firm in the same location. Other factors that play into higher fees are the cost of rent, salaries for support staff and firm "perks," or benefits.

Generally, fees are negotiable, although, as a rule, not after the services have been provided. If you intend to negotiate with your attorney for the value of the services provided, it would be best to initiate that conversation prior to the onset of the representation. Some attorneys may be offended by the notion they would consider negotiating their fees.

As with any other situation where you will be contracting for professional services, it is recommended you obtain, review and execute a fee agreement or engagement letter that clearly outlines the scope of the representation provided and the billing arrangement you've agreed to. Make sure you understand your rights with regard to termination of the relationship and what will happen in the event of a dispute between you and your attorney. Further, make sure you understand how long the attorney intends to maintain your file. Does the attorney have any processes or procedures for keeping you updated in the event the law changes with regard to the services that have previously been provided? Our experience is that most relationships with an attorney are based on a transactional basis. This means the legal relationship for representation purposes is terminated when the scope of the transaction is completed.

Other Helpful Suggestions

How do you locate the most qualified professional to serve as part of your team: This is a serious but not necessarily difficult task. First, consider recommendations from friends and other professionals. If you've identified one member of your team, they may be able to help you identify the remaining members. Personal referrals are generally the best way to find out about any type of professional service you might need, and financial, tax and legal representation is no exception. Talk to other people who are similarly situated. If you belong to any local organizations, consult with other members to obtain a referral. True professionals rely on good client relations and word-of-mouth reference for referral business. If you don't have any success getting a personal referral, consider local or state professional associations, your local estate planning council or other recognized referral services.

As a last resort, let your fingers do the walking and search your local yellow pages. However, understand that you should not select your trusted advisor based solely on yellow page advertising in the pertinent section— if such advertising is permitted in your state. You need to thoroughly consider to whom you should entrust your financial and estate planning.

Selecting the right team members is critical. However, just seeking a competent person and getting the right answers to your questions is often not enough. Consider the personal qualities your trusted advisor should have before you start interviewing candidates. Things you should look for:

▶ Scrupulous honesty and integrity
▶ Sensitive and perceptive communication
▶ Good judgment and common sense
▶ Discipline and toughness
▶ Creativity in finding constructive solutions
▶ Professional affiliations, designations, advanced training, specialization

Once you've identified a prospective team member, conduct an interview. Sit down with this individual and ask them questions pertinent to your areas of concern. Focus on the following:

▶ What is your experience in this field?
▶ Have you handled situations like mine?
▶ What are the possible problems or concerns for people like me?
▶ What is your planning process?
▶ How will you communicate with me?
▶ How often will we get together?
▶ Will you be my only contact, or will anyone else be working with you?
▶ Is there a charge for the initial consultation?
▶ Do you offer educational workshops?
▶ How do you handle your fees? Flat fee? Hourly? Commission?
▶ Beyond fees, what other types of expenses should I expect to incur?
▶ If I need to make changes, will there be an additional fee?
▶ When will I pay? How often will I receive a bill? If fees are not paid on time, will interest accrue?
▶ Will I sign a formal fee or engagement agreement?
▶ In the event of a dispute, do you recommend mediation, arbitration or litigation?
▶ How will you work with my other team members?

Other Things to Consider

Other things you should consider are the advisor's experience. The length of time the advisor has been in practice is an important indicator of his or her success and ability to adequately handle your financial or legal matter. Most professionals require between three and five years of experience before they have gained reasonable competence. Ask your advisor what they do to stay professionally competent? Do they attend a large number of continuing education programs or only enough to meet their professional requirements? Have they been given any awards? Do they teach locally, regionally or nationally? Are they published? A good indicator of a person's mastery of a subject is their ability to teach it or to write about it.

What is the individual's specific background or experiences that provide him or her with a unique perspective on your situation? Many advisors are "second career" individuals who may have worked in other professional areas prior to entering their current practice field. This past professional experience may be used to add significant expertise to their area of practice.

How does the advisor make you feel? Do you feel comfortable and understood? Do they speak in terms and use language you can understand? Does he or she take the time to explain those questions that are still unclear to you?

What is the advisor's current work load? Ask the advisor how many clients he or she is currently handling. Do they feel overwhelmed by their work load or outside commitments? How do they bring balance to their life? What are their outside interests or passions? Do you feel rushed? Are they taking the time to fully answer all questions regarding your situation? Are you feeling pressured to move forward and either engage the professional's services or buy something? Do you feel like you want to run out of the office? You may want to work only with people that you could consider as a friend. Life is too short to work with people that make you feel uncomfortable or that you don't like.

Ask your advisor about past results. Past results are never a guarantee of future success, but knowing an advisor's track record or experience in your type of situation can provide added comfort if he or she has had continuing success in situations similar in nature to yours.

Does your advisor have the ability to imagine ways in which something might go wrong? In the estate planning area, we incorporate a philosophy of "planning for the worst and hoping for the best" because any other kind of plan is simply wishful thinking. If something can go wrong it will, and Murphy's Law generally ensures that the one thing that was not planned for is the one thing that will happen. Make sure that your advisor is looking at all possible options, not just the most optimistic one.

Professional skill includes familiarity with the law, either estate planning or tax, as well as financial products and techniques. Skill cannot be taken for granted. Within the legal field, although different attorneys have different skills and skill levels, *any* attorney is legally permitted to handle any legal matter, so long as: 1) there is no conflict of interest; 2) the attorney can handle the matter competently (generally a matter of opinion—the attorney's); and 3) all other laws and rules of professional conduct are followed. These same rules generally apply to other professions as well.

Professional intuition, good character and an excellent reputation are also other traits that you should look for in a trusted advisor. Ultimately you must be comfortable with your choice of your advisor team—they can't help you if you can't or won't communicate with them. Choose people you respect, not someone who intimidates you or uses language or jargon that you don't understand. Look for someone who can make the complex simple. Find people that treat you the way you want to be treated, that answer your calls promptly and professionally. Do you feel at home when you visit their office? What sort of extras do they provide to cater to the individual or unique needs of their clients? Are you made to wait unnecessarily and for long periods of time?

To insure that you get good advice and have a great relationship with your trusted advisor team, consider the following thoughts and suggestions. Good professional assistance and advice is not a one-way street. You have to cooperate with your trusted advisors if you genuinely want him or her to help you. Generally your relationship with your advisor will be privileged and confidential, so you should be able to feel comfortable taking them into your confidence and revealing all of your pertinent information. Here are some important tips:

1) Don't withhold information from your advisor. If your advisor is expected to help you, it is important they know everything about you and your loved ones including all of your hopes, dreams, fears, aspirations, eccentricities and peccadilloes. Your advisor needs to know what it is like to be you or a member of your family. What does life look like for your loved ones if you are disabled or if you pass away? What assets do you own, how do you own them and who are the named beneficiaries? What type of planning have you done in the past? Without all of this information, the advisor will be unable to assess your situation, educate you about your options, and ultimately achieve a result that will be in your best interest.

2) Don't expect simple or immediate answers to complicated questions. Professionals are justifiably cautious in drawing conclusions or answering complex questions without consideration of all the relevant facts. A professional advisor knows there can be a number of answers to the same question and answers rarely fall into black and white categories. Your professional advisor has been trained to closely examine all of the facts before making recommendations. You may find that your advisors use words like, "it depends," "possibly," "could be" and "there is a great likelihood." Rarely will a professional make statements such as "guaranteed," "always" and "never." There are frequently a large number of factors that can cause any situation to have an unintended or unexpected outcome.

3) Keep your advisors informed of all new developments. In order to do a good job, your advisors need to be apprised of facts that may have changed in your personal or financial situation. When your advisor has all the facts, he or she can use this information to provide you with relevant information regarding changes in the financial landscape, new products, the law or changes in the advisor's professional experience.

4) Never hesitate to ask your advisor about anything you believe is relevant to your situation. Your advisor cannot read your mind. Also, remember that most financial and legal advisors are not psychiatrists, doctors or marriage counselors. You may still need other professionals to provide you with answers to all of your relevant questions and concerns.

5) Follow your advisor's advice. You asked for it. You paid good money for it. Don't work against the advice you've been given.

6) Be patient. Don't expect instant results. Trust your advisor to follow through and follow-up, but don't hesitate to ask for periodic progress reports. You have a right to know exactly what your advisor is doing for you. If you've engaged the services of a professional advisor who uses a formal planning process, you should always know what to expect next

7) Your advisor's primary duty is loyalty to you. His or her interest is achieving your goals and providing you with the highest possible quality of service. Early consultation with your advisor can save you trouble, time and money because:

- The solution to your current challenge may be easily resolved or prevented depending on the nature of your situation.
- The earlier you seek competent advice, the less time is generally needed to craft and complete a workable solution.

Information is generally more readily available when prompt action is taken. Within the financial and estate planning realm, this may be especially important in the event a person becomes mentally disabled, becomes catastrophically ill or dies before they have completed their planning. Many legal matters or strategies are time sensitive or may have a statute of limitations. Failure to act in a timely manner may prevent you from acting at all.

The people that will comprise your trusted advisor team are going to be some of the most important people in your life. This is not an area in which to skimp or accept anything but the best. Build a team you can trust and you can and will accomplish your goals. ❈

chapter ten

Resources

A

A Guide to Recalling and Telling Your Life Story
Hospice Foundation of America 800-854-3402 www.hospicefoundation.org

American Association of Retired Persons (AARP)—*www.aarp.org*

American Bankruptcy Institute—*www.abiworld.org*

American Council of Life Insurance—*www.acli.com*

American Institute of CPAs (AICPA)—*www.aicpa.org*

Association for Pet Loss and Bereavement (APLB)—*www.aplb.org*

American Red Cross—*www.redcross.org*

B

Better Business Bureau—*www.bbb.org*

C

Caring Connections—*www.caringinfo.org*

Certified Financial Planner Board of Standards, Inc.—*www.cfp.net*

D

Docubank—*www.Docubank.com*

F

Financial Planning Association—*www.fpanet.org*

Funeral poems, songs, eulogies and creative ideas:
www.memorialserviceplanning.com

Funeral Consumer Allianc—*www.funeral.org*

H

HAHN & POLLOCK, LLC.—*www. HAHNPOLLOCK.com*

Home for Life—*www.homeforlife.org*

Hoyt & Bryan, LLC—*www.HoytBryan.com*

I

Institute for Divorce Financial Analysts—*www.InstituteDFA.com*

Internal Revenue Service—*www.irs.gov*

L

Living With the End in Mind: A Practical Checklist for Living Life to the Fullest by Embracing Your Mortality by Erin Tierney Kramp—*www.careofdying.org*

M

My Personal Wishes—*www.MyPersonalWishes.com*

N

National Association of Estate Planners and Councils—*www.naepc.org*

National Association of Investment Clubs—*www.betterinvesting.org*

National Association of Social Security Claimant Representatives (NOSSCR)—*www.nosscr.org*

National Foundation for Credit Counseling—*www.debtadvice.org*

National Network of Estate Planning Attorneys—*www.nnepa.com*

P

Pet Guardian—www.PetGuardian.com

R

Rainbow Bridge—*www.rainbowbridge.com*

S

Security and Exhange Commission—*www.sec.gov*

Small Business Administration—*www.sba.gov*

Social Security Administration—*www.ssa.gov*

Sunbridge—*www.sunbridgestrategies.com*

T

The Financial Planning Association—*www.fpanet.org*

The Five Wishes—*www.agingwithdignity.org*

U

U.S. Department of Labor—Employee Benefits—*www.dol.gov*

V

Values history form—*www.unm.edu*

W

Wealthcounsel—*www.wealthcounsel.com*

Women's Institute for Financial Education—*www.wife.org*

Women in Transition—Navigating the Financial and Legal Challenges in Your Life by Peggy R. Hoyt and Candace M. Pollock—*www.WomenInTransitionToday.com*

Other Books by Peggy and Candace:

All My Children Wear Fur Coats –How to Leave a Legacy for Your Pet—www.LegacyForYourPet.com

Special People Special Planning—Creating a Safe Legal Haven for Families with Special Needs—www.SpecialPeopleSpecialPlanning.com

Loving Without a License—A Survival Guide for Same Sex Couples and Unmarried Partners—www.LovingWithoutALicense.com

A Matter of Trust—The Importance of Personal Instructions—www.AMatterOfTrust.info

Appendix A
(top ten estate planning mistakes)

MISTAKE #1: Waiting Too Long

You are not a procrastinator. You've created your professional advisor team and have a working financial plan and up-to-date estate plan.

► You've avoided the following pitfalls:
  • *"When* I win the lottery and *if* I die" mentality—which is more likely to occur?
  • 55% of Americans have no Will or other directives to specify who gets their "stuff" when they die
  • 70% have no provisions for minor or disabled children
  • 67% have no Living Will or other healthcare proxies
  • 95% have no financial powers of attorney

► The state has a plan if you fail to provide your own directives
  • Death or "living" probate (guardianship)
  • Terry Schiavo's case has led many states to amend their laws

► Penny-wise and pound-foolish?
  • More likely to get cost-effective options & advice when planning is not done under crisis conditions

MISTAKE #2: Self-diagnosing & Self-treating

You do not self-diagnose or self-treat. You realize that professionals can and do add value for the services they provide. You make sound decisions and know how to execute them. Congratulations, you've assimilated the following:

► **Good news**: Legal & financial professionals no longer have monopoly on "special knowledge". Savvy consumers can identify and compare services/product they think they need and options/costs via internet.

► **Bad news**: Consumers can confuse lots of information with "wisdom". Competition for consumer dollars drives down legal & financial service costs, leading consumers to believe that "It can't be that difficult if it is that cheap!" and that estate planning is an easy "do-it-yourself" task.

► Professionals know the questions to ask and know scope of available options; have methods and experience to make sure nothing is overlooked.

► Amateurs: Will likely get amateur results that can have huge ramifications—immediately and for generations.

MISTAKE #3: Planning for Death But Not Incapacity

Your comprehensive estate plan includes directives for health care and incapacity, not just setting forth your wishes in the event of death. You have realized the following:

► Mental incapacity is more likely than death between ages 30-70. However, most people don't have *financial* powers of attorney

► You need to authorize someone to act for you when you cannot speak for yourself:
  • Living Will & Durable Healthcare Power of Attorney (DHCPOA) do **not** authorize agents to handle financial matters
  • Guardianship gives legal authority to handle disabled loved one's financial matters but must comply with state probate laws (law gives priority to blood relatives)
  • <u>Durable</u> financial powers of attorney (DFPOA) can avert need for guardianship

► Durable Financial Power of Attorney (DFPOA) features to consider for a "custom fit" for your needs
  • Should it give the agent general or limited authority to act? (special language is needed for special circumstances)
  • Should it have immediate effect or "springing" effect when a particular event occurs?

- Should it give unlimited or limited authority to make gifts and should this include gifts to the agent himself? (amount & recipients—important for Medicaid planning)
- Should you name dual agents or alternate agents?

MISTAKE #4: Thwarting Goals with Beneficiary Forms

You realize that beneficiary designations are critical to an estate plan and these must be coordinated with your will and/or trust documents. You regularly meet with your advisors to review all your assets to make sure they are consistent with your written instructions for disability and death. You acknowledged the following:

▶ Simplicity of beneficiary forms can lead you to believe they don't require the same attention to detail you devote to rest of estate plan. **But,** because they automatically direct the asset to the named beneficiary, make sure you pay close attention to their role in achieving your overall goals.

▶ Estate planning goals can be thwarted when:
- First beneficiary dies before or with the asset owner and no secondary beneficiary is named

▶ Asset must go through probate (Will or "no Will")
- Designation directs assets outright to minor or disabled beneficiaries who can be vulnerable to exploitation or ineligible for public-assistance programs
- Don't address competing interests of second spouse and children from prior relationship; e.g., second spouse who is named as 100% primary beneficiary and has no legal obligation or mechanism to honor promises to take care of deceased's children from prior marriage.

MISTAKE #5: Underestimating Jointly Titled Assets

You know that jointly titled assets can often be a trap for the unwary. You've carefully examined all of your assets to make sure that jointly titled assets are consistent with your estate plan and your goals. You understand that:

- ▶ Joint ownership is often chosen to avoid probate and to protect owners' mutual interests in property – especially for unmarried couples

- ▶ Joint Tenant's with Rights of Survivorship (JTWROS) is not the same thing as Joint Tenants (JT) —make sure you understand which one you have

- ▶ Less familiar and potentially bad features of JTWROS:
  - Asset is available to creditors of *all* joint owners (divorce/failed business/illness)
  - One joint owner can withdraw all funds *w/o* asking for permission of the other joint owner (e.g., divorce)
  - **But** a joint owner requires consent of other joint owners to sell

- ▶ Problems: if joint owner disagrees or is incapacitated
  - No way to hold asset in trust for benefit of disabled joint owner
  - Survivor-owner might not have liquid assets to pay applicable estate taxes
  - Can trigger gift tax consequences when unmarried joint owners don't contribute equal amounts to acquire asset

- ▶ JTWROS provisions can place too many assets directly into name of surviving owner and thwart owners' intention to reduce estate taxes

MISTAKE #6: Not Using Insurance Effectively

Your investment advisor has educated you about the benefits of insurance products and the value they add to your financial and estate plan. You aren't insurance poor but have used it to supplement your savings, replace lost income or create wealth (to cover taxes and/or provide liquid assets for survivors) at the time of your death. You know that:

- ▶ Just like Wills or Trusts, insurance is an estate-planning tool that can protect the people and things you cherish. It leverages small sums (premiums) to *create* wealth and/or to *protect* assets from loss due to:
  - **Death**– replace breadwinner earnings/homemaker contributions, covering costs of last illness, funeral and probate, taxes, mortgages and college

- **Disability**– cover nursing-home costs, loss of income or payments to those who must perform tasks disabled person used to do
- **Property Loss**– (damage, destruction or theft) loss of use & replacement costs
- **Unemployment**– offsets loss of income, moving & retraining expenses
- **Liability**– to protect future security and assets earmarked for things such as retirement or college costs.

MISTAKE #7: Lacking Liquidity

You have plenty of liquidity in your financial and estate plan. Important assets will not have to be sold in order to pay taxes or provide distributions to beneficiaries. Liquidity can be created in a variety of ways—you know this is important because

▶ You don't want your heirs to lose their intended legacy, reduce their inheritance or lose control if no liquidity

▶ Liquidity is the ease with which assets can be converted into cash without a significant loss of value or delay

▶ Insurance is the traditional way to create liquidity (cash) to cover estate taxes or other costs at death to avoid unplanned use of other assets. But other assets can be earmarked to serve this role, if they are sufficiently liquid.

▶ Bottom line: Remember to plan for liquidity. This is especially important for business owners, unmarried couples and people with estates over $2,000,000 (under current federal estate tax levels; some states have their own estate tax levels)

MISTAKE #8: Failing to Take Holistic View

You realize that estate planning requires a holistic view that takes all aspects of your financial life into consideration. You have learned that:

▶ Assets fall into 1 of 3 categories that control transfer at death:

- **Probate**
  - Will or "no will" probate (intestate succession)
  - Asset in single name with <u>no</u> built-in survivorship instructions;
  - Ex.: House in your name only
- **Operation of Law**
  - State authorized categories of property with built-in survivor ship instructions;
  - Ex.: Joint Tenants w/Rights of Survivorship (JTWROS) property or Transfer on Death (TOD) property
- **Contract**
  - Terms of contract set forth survivorship instructions
  - Ex.: Retirement accounts or Payable on Death (POD) bank accounts

▶ Review all asset classes with same level of attention you use when preparing a Will to make sure the directives for other categories are properly completed and don't conflict with your overall goals.

▶ A Will is *powerless* over property that is transferred by Operation of Law or by Contract provisions *unless* the named survivor-beneficiary predeceases owner or there is a defect in designation form. A will is always a good "safety net" for such situations. It "catches" any assets that fall through the other instructions you set forth.

MISTAKE #9: Failing to Leave a Paper Trail

You keep good records and are organized. You review your financial and estate planning documents on an annual basis to make sure they are an accurate reflection of your current financial and family situation; that they are consistent with changes in the law; changes in your lawyer's experience and changes in the way you want to leave a legacy. You know that:

▶ Legal directives must be *available* if they are to do any good when needed.
  - Especially in urgent medical situations

▶ Spare heirs/agents struggles with remembering what you own, where assets are held and where your directives for each asset might be.

► Create a "Location List": Keep it simple but updated with copies to advisors or agents so they know your wishes.
  • List all directives you created along with dates: This includes Will/Trust, deeds, powers of attorney, healthcare proxies, beneficiary-designation forms, payable-on-death accounts, insurance policies, burial contracts, safe deposit boxes/keys, safes, employment or veterans benefits, debts, etc.
  • List location of originals and who has copies (in case you need to revoke or amend)
  • List names and numbers for your primary healthcare providers, legal & financial advisors, insurance agent and accountant. Include names of agents or family or others who should be contacted in the event of your disability or death.

MISTAKE #10: Failing to Keep the Plan Current

► You meet with your advisors on a regular and predetermined basis to make sure that your plan remains current. This is important to you because:
  • Once is not enough! Plans should be reviewed and updated to maintain a good "fit"

► 3 areas of change can threaten your original plan
  • Changes in family and financial situation
  • Changes in law (state & federal)
  • Changes in advisor experience and strategies

► A formal updating system makes sure you take advantage of changes and avoid threats to your plan.

Appendix B
(estate planning checklist)

Part 1—Communicating Your Wishes

☐ Yes ☐ No   Do you have a will or trust?

☐ Yes ☐ No   Are you comfortable with the executor(s) or trustee(s) you have selected?

☐ Yes ☐ No   Have you executed a living will or healthcare proxy in the event of catastrophic illness or disability? Are your important family members named in these documents as your surrogate for decision making purposes?

☐ Yes ☐ No   Have you executed a durable financial power of attorney for the purpose of appointing an agent to handle your financial affairs in the event of your disability?

☐ Yes ☐ No   Have you considered a revocable living trust to consolidate assets, avoid probate, minimize exposure to estate tax and provide long-term protections for your spouse and other loved ones?

☐ Yes ☐ No   If you have a living trust, have you titled your assets in the name of the trust? Have you named your trust as the primary beneficiary on your contract assets such as insurance, annuities, and retirement plans.

☐ Yes ☐ No   If you have a will, trust or other legal directives, have they been reviewed in the last two years to ensure they are consistent with your wishes, the status of the law and your attorney's changing experience?

Part 2—Protecting Your Family

☐ Yes ☐ No   Does your will name a guardian for your minor children?

☐ Yes ☐ No   Does your estate plan specifically include provisions to protect your spouse and other loved ones in the event of your death?

☐ Yes ☐ No   Are you sure you have the right amount and type of life insurance to help with survivor income, loan repayment, capital needs and estate-settlement expenses?

☐ Yes ☐ No   Have you considered an irrevocable life insurance trust to exclude the insurance proceeds from being taxed as part of your estate?

☐ Yes ☐ No   Have you considered creating trusts for either your spouse, partner or other family to facilitate gift giving?

Part 3—Helping to Reduce Your Estate and Income Taxes

☐ Yes ☐ No   Do you and your spouse each individually own enough assets for each of you to qualify for the applicable exclusion amount, currently $1.5 million?

☐ Yes ☐ No   Are both your estate plan and your spouse's designed to take advantage of each of your applicable exclusion amounts, currently $1.5 million?

☐ Yes ☐ No   Are you making gifts to family members or others that take advantage of the annual gift tax exclusion, currently $11,000?

☐ Yes ☐ No   Have you gifted assets with a strong probability of future appreciation in order to maximize future estate tax savings?

☐ Yes ☐ No   Have you considered charitable trusts that can provide you with both estate and income tax benefits?

Part 4—Protecting Your Business

☐ Yes ☐ No   If you own a business, do you have a management succession plan?

☐ Yes ☐ No   Do you have a buy-sell agreement for your family business interests?

☐ Yes ☐ No   Is your spouse employed by your business? Have you taken all steps necessary to ensure his or her continued participation in the business in the event of your death?

☐ Yes ☐ No   Have you considered a gift program that involves your family-owned business?

COORDINATE YOUR DIRECTIVES TO CONTROL YOUR ASSETS

PROBATE	OPERATION OF LAW	CONTRACT
WILL "NO WILL PROBATE" [intestate succession = state's probate laws say who gets what]	JTWROS TBE TOD	INSURANCE POD RETIREMENT ACCOUNTS IRAs TRUSTS
Only controls assets that are 1.) titled in your individual name and 2.) that have no built-in survivorship feature.	Has built-in survivorship feature that tells who gets the asset at owner's death. **WARNING!** If there is a defect in title, asset must go through probate to decide who gets asset under will or "no will" probate.	Has built-in survivorship feature that tells who gets the asset at owner's death. **WARNING!** If there is a defect in beneficiary designation(s), the asset might have to go through probate to decide who gets the asset under the will or "no will" probate if the terms of the contract don't have a default recipient provision.
	Go to probate if defect in designation.	Go to probate if defect in designation.

DISABILITY DIRECTIVES

WHAT ARE YOUR INSTRUCTIONS?

WHO IS AUTHORIZED TO SPEAK & ACT FOR YOU WHEN YOU ARE UNABLE TO
COMMUNICATE YOUR WISHES?

HEALTH	FINANCES
♦ Living Will	♦ Durable Financial Power of Attorney
♦ Durable Healthcare Power of Attorney	♦ Alternate or Dual Agent(s)?
♦ HIPAA	♦ General or limited powers?
♦ Durable Mental Healthcare Power of Attorney	♦ Springing or Immediate Effect?
	♦ Unlimited or Limited Gifting Powers?
♦ Organ Donation Form	
♦ Living Trust	♦ Living Trust
♦ Guardian Nomination (for yourself)	
Default plan, if you don't make one: State laws/court.	Default plan, if you don't make one: State laws/court.

Other Considerations:

Where to keep originals?
Only useful if available. Copies & repositories [e.g., Docubank, www.docubank.com].

Paper trail: Location list.

Amendments and revocation.

GLOSSARY
(financial planning terms)

ANNUAL PERCENTAGE RATE (APR)—A loan's yearly rate of interest. The Consumer Credit Protection Act of 1968 requires lenders to
calculate this figure in a standardized way and disclose it to consumers.

ANNUITY—A contract under which one party pays money (lump sum or
period payments) to an insurance company in exchange for the company's
promise to pay the party a specific amount of money over her lifetime.
Annuities can be for fixed periods or for the lifetime of one or more people. Payments to survivors will continue to survivors of annuitants for the
remainder of the fixed period. Surrender fees may apply if the investor
cancels the investment contract before the end of the fixed period.
Lifetime annuities continue for the annuitant's lifetime but do not pay
income to survivors.

ASSET—Anything owned by a person that has value. This could be cash,
investments, real property, automobiles.

BANKRUPTCY—A court declaration that a person is financially insolvent.

BUY-SELL AGREEMENT—A contract sets forth the terms of the sale of
business interests under specified circumstances. Normally used among
owners to provide liquidity and to replace lost income to the owners
and/or their survivors due to the death, disability, retirement, exit from the
business or from creditor attachment, or divorce.

BOND—An "IOU" debt issued by a corporation or government entity in
exchange for interest paid to investors who buy the debt.

CAPITAL GAINS or LOSS—The profit or loss on the sale of an asset.
Gains are taxed at different levels depending on whether they are short-
term (sales of investments that are made w/i 1 yr. acquiring the asset) or
long-term (held at least 1 yr.)

CASH SURRENDER VALUE—The amount an insurance policy owner could receive if she cashed in certain types of insurance policies. Some policies have no cash value; e.g. TERM INSURANCE.

CERTIFICATE OF DEPOSIT—A savings bank with a financial institution where the investor agrees to leave the funds in the account for a specified time period and the financial institution pays interest at a higher rate than on accounts where the investor can remove the funds at any time. A penalty fee is assessed if the investor cashes in the CD prior to the contract date.

DIVIDENDS—A portion of net profits paid by companies to stockholders or interest paid on savings, money market mutual funds or the refund of excess premiums from a whole life insurance policy.

DOLLAR-COST AVERAGING—A method for averaging purchase prices of investment shares. The investor invests the same dollar amount at each purchase interval regardless of the price of the shares. This method helps the buyer purchase more shares at low prices than at high prices, making the average price for all shares lower overall.

EQUITY—The difference between an asset's value and the debt on it.

EXPENSE RATIO—The ratio of a mutual fund's annual operating expenses to its average net assets (annual operating expenses ÷ average net assets in the fund).

INSURANCE—Adjustable Life Insurance—Insurance that allows the owner to increase or decrease the premium, face value, coverage period and/or period over which premiums are paid. It has similarities to Universal Life and Whole Life policies.

Term Life Insurance—Insurance that provides a lump sum payment to beneficiaries if the insured dies within a specified period (the term), such as 5 years or 10 years. When the term expires, the protection expires.

Whole Life Insurance—Life insurance that provides a lump sum payment to beneficiaries over the insured's lifetime. Premiums and death benefits are level for the life of the policy. Cash value accrues under the policy which is available to the owner for loans or at termination of the contract.

IRREVOCABLE LIFE INSURANCE TRUST—A trust created for the purpose of receiving or purchasing life insurance payable to trust beneficiaries at the insured's death. The trust is irrevocable to avoid having the policy value included in an individual's gross taxable estate at death.

MONEY MARKET FUNDS—Mutual funds invested in high-yield money market instruments.

RISK TOLERANCE—An investor's ability and willingness to accept a given level and type of risk associated with an investment.

TOTAL PORTFOLIO RISK—The entire risk associated with a portfolio. This includes systematic risk (risk associated with broad economic or political influences that affect most similar investments) and unsystematic risk (risk associated with factors unique to a company or industry such as market demand or costs of raw materials). Systematic risk cannot be diversified since it affects the system as a whole. Unsystematic risk can be diversified by investing in companies that are not subject to the same categories of risks overall, such as costs of raw materials, durable consumer products or labor requirements.

GLOSSARY
(ESTATE PLANNING TERMS)

ADMINISTRATOR — Person named by the court to administer a probate estate. Also called an Executor or Personal Representative.

AGENT — An individual named in a power of attorney with authority to act on the power giver's behalf. Has a fiduciary responsibility to the power giver.

ANCILLARY ADMINISTRATION — An additional probate in another state. Typically required when you own assets or real estate in a state other than the state where you live that is not titled in the name of your trust or in the name of a joint owner with rights of survivorship.

BASIS — What you paid for an asset. Value used to determine gain or loss for capital gains and income tax purposes.

BUY-SELL AGREEMENT — A written agreement between co-owners of a business to determine the rights of the owners in the event of retirement, disability or death.

CO-TRUSTEES — Two or more individuals who have been named to act together in managing a trust's assets. A Corporate Trustee can also be a Co-Trustee.

CORPORATE TRUSTEE — An institution, such as a bank or trust company, that specializes in managing or administering trusts.

DISCLAIM — To refuse to accept a gift or inheritance so it may be transferred to the next recipient in line. Must be done within nine months of the date-of-death.

DURABLE POWER OF ATTORNEY FOR FINANCIAL MATTERS — A legal document that gives another person full or limited legal authority to make financial decisions on your behalf in your absence. Valid through mental incapacity. Ends at revocation, adjudication of incapacity or death.

DURABLE POWER OF ATTORNEY FOR HEALTHCARE — A legal document that gives another person legal authority to make health care decisions for you if you are unable to make them for yourself. Also called Healthcare Proxy, Healthcare Surrogate or Medical Power of Attorney.

ESTATE ADMINISTRATION — The process of settling either a probate estate or trust estate. There are generally three steps that include identifying the assets, paying the debts of the estate and distributing the balance to the beneficiaries.

EXECUTOR — Another name for Personal Representative.

FIDUCIARY — Person having the legal duty to act for another person's benefit. Requires great confidence, trust, and a high degree of good faith. Usually associated with a Trustee or Personal Representative.

FUNDING — The process of re-titling and transferring your assets to your Living Trust. Also includes the re-designation of beneficiaries to include your Living Trust as a beneficiary. Sometimes called asset integration.

INTER VIVOS — Latin term that means "between the living." An inter vivos trust is created while you are living instead of after you die. A Revocable Living Trust is an inter vivos trust.

IRREVOCABLE LIFE INSURANCE TRUST (ILIT) — An irrevocable trust for the purpose of holding title to life insurance. Used as an advance planning technique to remove the death benefit proceeds of life insurance from an insured's gross taxable estate.

IRREVOCABLE TRUST — A trust that cannot be changed or canceled once it is set up. Opposite of Revocable Living Trust. Can be created during lifetime or after death.

INTESTATE — Dying without a Will.

JOINT OWNERSHIP — When two or more persons own the same asset.

Joint Tenants with Right of Survivorship — A form of joint ownership where the deceased owner's share automatically and immediately transfers to the surviving joint tenant(s) or owner(s).

LIVING TRUST — A legal entity created during your life, to which you transfer ownership of your assets. Contains your instructions to control and manage your assets while you are alive and well, plan for you and your loved ones in the event of your mental disability and give what you have, to whom you want, when you want, the way you want at your death. Avoids guardianship of the property and probate only if fully funded at incapacity and/or death. Also called a Revocable Inter Vivos Trust.

LIFE ALLIANCE AGREEMENT — A written agreement between two life alliance partners for the purpose of establishing ownership to property, rights and obligations with regard to property and disposition of property in the event of the termination of the relationship.

LIFE ALLIANCE PARTNER — A life partner of the same or opposite-sex in a committed relationship.

LIMITED LIABILITY COMPANY (LLC) — A form of legal entity that can provide limited liability from the claims of creditors. Can be taxed as a sole proprietorship, partnership, s-corporation or c-corporation.

LIVING WILL — A legal document that sets forth your wishes regarding the termination of life-prolonging procedures if you are mentally incapacitated and your illness or injury is expected to result in your death.

PERSONAL REPRESENTATIVE — Another name for an Executor or Administrator.

POUR OVER WILL — An abbreviated Will used with a Living Trust. It sets forth your instructions regarding guardianship of minor children and the transfer (pour over) of all assets owned in your individual name (probate assets) to your Living Trust.

POWER OF ATTORNEY — A legal document that gives another person legal authority to act on your behalf for a stated purpose. Ends at revocation, incapacity (unless it is a durable power of attorney) or death.

PROBATE — The legal process of validating a Will, paying debts, and distributing assets after death. Generally requires the serves of an attorney.

PROBATE ESTATE — The assets owned in your individual name at death (or beneficiary designations payable to your estate). Does not include assets owned as joint tenants with rights of survivorship, payable-on-death accounts, insurance payable to a named beneficiary or trust, and other assets with beneficiary designations.

PROBATE FEES — Legal, executor, court, and appraisal fees for an estate that requires probate. Probate fees are paid from assets in the estate before the assets are fully distributed to the heirs.

REVOCABLE LIVING TRUST — Another name for a Living Trust.

SPENDTHRIFT CLAUSE — Protects assets in a Trust from a beneficiary's creditors.

SUCCESSOR TRUSTEE — Person or institution named in a trust document that will take over should the first Trustee die, resign or otherwise become unable to act.

TESTAMENTARY TRUST — A Trust created in a Will. Can only go into effect at death. Does not avoid probate.

TESTATE — An estate where the decedent died with a valid Will.

TRUST ADMINISTRATION — The legal process required to administer trust assets after incapacity or death. Includes the management of trust assets for the named beneficiaries, the payment of debts, taxes or other expenses and the distribution of assets to beneficiaries according to the Trust instructions. Generally requires the services of an attorney.

TRUSTEE — Person or institution who manages and distributes another's assets according to the instructions in the Trust document.

WILL (OR LAST WILL & TESTAMENT) — A written document with instructions for disposing of assets after death. A Will can only be enforced through the probate court.

About the Authors

 **PEGGY R. HOYT, J.D., M.B.A.** Peggy is the oldest of four daughters born to John and Trudy Hoyt. She was born in Dearborn, Michigan, and spent her first ten years as a "PK," or "preacher's kid," before her father joined The Humane Society of the United States. Peggy graduated with an A.A. degree from Marymount University in Arlington, Virginia; earned a B.B.A. and M.B.A. from Stetson University in DeLand, Florida; and earned a J.D. from Stetson University College of Law in St. Petersburg, Florida.

After receiving her M.B.A., Peggy worked as a financial consultant for Merrill Lynch. Today, Peggy and her law partner, Randy Bryan, own and operate Hoyt & Bryan, LLC, in Oviedo, Florida. Their law firm limits its practice to estate planning and administration for individuals, married couples and life alliance partners, including special needs planning, pet planning, elder law and guardianships. She also works in the areas of business creation, succession and exit planning, as well as real estate, corporate and equine law.

She is active in a variety of organizations, including the National Network of Estate Planning Attorneys, Wealth Counsel, Sunbridge Strategies and serves on the board of the Central Florida Estate Planning Council. She is a regular speaker on team training and estate planning topics and is also a contributor of practice management materials. In addition, she serves as trustee to Stetson University's Business School Foundation.

Peggy's passion is her pets that inspired her one-of-a kind book called *All My Children Wear Fur Coats – How to Leave a Legacy for Your Pet,* (*www.LegacyForYourPet.com*). She enjoys spending her "free" time with her husband, Joe Allen; riding or playing with her wild mustang horses, Reno and Tahoe, and Premarin rescue, Sierra; walking her dogs, Kira, Corkie, Tiger and Fiona and Leiden; and hanging out with her cats, Beijing, Bangle, Cuddles, Tommy and Shamu.

CANDACE M. POLLOCK, J.D. Prior to attending law school, Candace owned a business that provided claims review and consulting services to Ohio lawyers in the area of workers' compensation and Social Security claims—areas involving the rights of people with disabilities. During this period she was a founding member and first acting president of the Women Business Owners' Association (now known as the Cleveland Chapter of the National Association of Women Business Owners). She graduated from Cleveland-Marshall Law School and is a principal in HAHN & POLLOCK, LLC.

Candace continued to represent the interests of people with disabilities while expanding her practice to include estate and financial planning, probate and elder law services in response to the needs of her clients. Her practice focuses on the unique planning needs of unmarried partners, the disabled and the elderly.

Her participation in professional and community activities includes leadership roles in legal and professional associations: Chair of the Workers' Compensation and Social Security Section of the Cuyahoga County Bar Association, Representative-at-Large on the Board of Trustees of the Ohio Academy of Trial Lawyers (OATL) and Member of the Executive Committee of the Workers' Compensation Section of OATL. She is a former mentor-coach with the National Network of Estate Planning Attorneys' Practice Builder Program and contributing editor of The Daily Plan-it, a newsletter to the legal and financial planning community. She participates in non-board positions in charitable and political organizations.

In addition to her professional and community advocacy activities, she is a national and local speaker and writer on topics associated with estate and disability planning. This is her fourth book.

Candace resides in Cleveland, OH with her life alliance partner, Hutch, and their family of animals.

Contact Us

Peggy and Candace are available as speakers and for interviews and are happy to contribute written material to publications regarding planning for life alliance partners. Please feel free to contact them at:

HOYT & BRYAN, LLC	**HAHN & POLLOCK, LLC**
254 Plaza Drive	**820 West Superior Avenue, Suite 510**
Oviedo, Florida 32765	**Cleveland, Ohio 44113**
(407) 977-8080 (T)	**(216) 861-6160 (T)**
(407) 977-8078 (F)	**(216) 861-5272 (F)**
peggy@HoytBryan.com	**info@HAHNPOLLOCK.com**
www.HoytBryan.com	**www.HAHNPOLLOCK.com**

Other Planning Concerns:

Pets. For information related to planning for your pets, please visit www.LegacyForYourPet.com

Special Needs. If you have a special needs family member, please visit www.SpecialPeopleSpecialPlanning.com.

Unmarried Couples. Contact us at www.LovingWithoutALicense.com.

Personalzed Instructions. To supplement your legal instructions with personalized instructions, visit www.AMatterOfTrust.info

Printed in the United States
211901BV00001B/7/A